BRITISH ECONOMIC HISTORY ★ A Garland Series

Edited by
PETER MATHIAS
Oxford University
and
STUART BRUCHEY
Columbia University

THE IMPACT OF INDUSTRIALIZATION ON AN URBAN LABOR MARKET ★ Birmingham, England 1770–1860

Ed Duggan

Garland Publishing, Inc.
New York & London ★ 1985

Library of Congress Cataloging-in-Publication Data

Duggan, Ed, 1945–
The impact of industrialization on an urban labor market.

(British economic history)
Thesis (Ph.D.)—University of Wisconsin-Madison, 1972.
Bibliography: p.
1. Birmingham (West Midlands, England)—Industries—History. 2. Birmingham (West Midlands, England)—Economic conditions. 3. Labor supply—England—Birmingham (West Midlands)—History. I. Title. II. Series.
HC258.B6D84 1985 338.09424′96 84-46000
ISBN 0-8240-6680-4

All volumes in this series are printed on acid-free, 250-year-life paper.

Printed in the United States of America

THE IMPACT OF INDUSTRIALIZATION ON AN URBAN LABOR MARKET: BIRMINGHAM, ENGLAND, 1770-1860

EDWARD P. DUGGAN

Dissertation accepted by the University of Wisconsin-Madison, in 1972, for the degree of Doctor of Philosophy (History).

TABLE OF CONTENTS

	Pages
PREFACE I	iv
PREFACE II	v
CHAPTER I: INTRODUCTION	1
CHAPTER 2: ECONOMIC HISTORY OF BIRMINGHAM	17
Birmingham at the beginning of the Industrial Revolution: 1777	17
Birmingham during the Industrial Revolution: 1777 - 1830	25
Birmingham after the Industrial Revolution: 1830 - 1860	32
CHAPTER 3: BIRMINGHAM ENTREPRENEURS AND THE INDUSTRIALIZING EXPERIENCE	40
Sources and Costs of Capital	45
Fixed and Working Capital	62
CHAPTER 4: BIRMINGHAM LABOR AND THE INDUSTRIALIZING EXPERIENCE	77
Definition of Specific Labor Forces to be Compared	77
Skilled Workers: Quality and Quantity	94
Definition and Identification of Skilled Workers	94
Technological Change	111
Wages	120
Trade Unions	135
Employment and Income Stability	145
Summary and Conclusions	153
CHAPTER 5: SOURCES OF LABOR, TRAINING, AND EDUCATION	156
Sources of Labor	156
Training	162
Education	178

	Pages
CHAPTER 6: SERVICES IN THE BIRMINGHAM ECONOMY	183
General Role of Services	183
Role of Services in Birmingham	188
CHAPTER 7: URBAN-INDUSTRIAL GROWTH AND LABOR FORCE RECRUITMENT IN BIRMINGHAM: SOME CONCLUDING COMMENTS	200
APPENDIX	209
Labor Costs	210
BIBLIOGRAPHY	217

PREFACE I

A phenomenon of continuing fascination, the industrial revolution in Great Britain has beguiled scholars for years with its complexity. This study seeks to incorporate a new dimension, space, by focussing on workers in urban areas. With a clearer picture of how people in different areas responded to the process of industrial change, with all its variants, we might better understand the impact of these forces on ourselves today.

To accomplish even this limited task, many minds were needed - for construction, interpretation, criticism, and insight. Staffs working with many collections, but particularly at the Birmingham Reference Library and the University of Birmingham, provided considerable assistance. Individuals who have shown much generosity with their time include Morton Rothstein, Peter Lindert, Eugene Smolensky, Rondo Cameron, and many others who engaged in conversation and debate, especially in the Economic History Workshop at the University of Wisconsin.

The most valuable aid has been my wife, Sharon, who has carried the anguish and excitement of dissertation writing with enviable grace, and who has consistently shown an intriguing capacity to distinguish the fine line separating wisdom from witlessness. To her I dedicate this work. (1972)

PREFACE II

Because of the peculiar needs of the publishing moment, my wife, Sharon, again typed this dissertation. It is virtually unaltered from the original. Not so her grace and judgement, however, which continue to grow without measure. (1984)

CHAPTER ONE: INTRODUCTION

Despite much scholarly interest, the industrial revolution remains unexamined in several respects. Few students have failed to mention the increase in urban population during the period, for example, but even fewer have specified precise relationships between the intermixed processes of urbanization and industrialization.

Several theories have evolved to explain urban growth itself: central place theory, which stresses the role of a center in providing services to surrounding areas; location theory, which argues that cities providing the lowest total cost to the most firms will grow largest; and export base theory, which argues that linkages with other industries and services cause cities to grow as their export bases grow.[1] Each theory provides useful insights, but none completely explains the growth of many cities and a single city often fits all three explanations well.

---

[1] See for each theory the following respectively: Brian J. L. Berry, Geography of Market Centers and Retail Distribution, Prentice-Hall, Englewood, N. J., 1967; E. M. Hoover, The Location of Economic

Although natural increase plays a role, most cities grow relatively larger and more quickly than others mainly by attracting entrepreneurs and workers from other areas. Thus, as Redford has noted, the great cities of the industrial north in England expanded by recruiting entrepreneurs and workers from nearby farms and villages.[2]

Grasping for markers, historians have often focussed on single variables, like transportation or raw material supply, holding all others constant, to steer them through the tangle of reasons for urban-industrial growth.[3] As the critical factor in urban growth and a key factor in industrial growth, labor supply has attracted much scrutiny, but with inconclusive results.

Activity, McGraw-Hill, N.Y., 1948; W.P. Thompson, A Preface to Urban Economics, Johns Hopkins Press, Baltimore, 1965. See also the review article by Eric Lampard in H.S. Perloff, L. Wingo, eds., Issues in Urban Economics, Johns Hopkins Press, Baltimore, 1968, 81-139.

[2] A. Redford, Labour Migration in England 1800-1850, 2nd. edn. 1926, edited and revised by W. Chaloner, A. Kelley, N.Y., 1968, 183.

[3] A broader case is made in M. J. Wise, "Some Factors Influencing the Growth of Birmingham," Geography Vol. 33, 1948, 183; and M. J. Wise, B. L. C. Johnson, "The Changing Regional Pattern during the Eighteenth Century," Birmingham and Its

C. P. Kindleberger, for example, has argued the case for cheap labor in stimulating growth but H. J. Habakkuk has argued precisely the opposite.[4] Providing fresh insightful opinion in a difficult area of investigation, both scholars show, by their contradiction, how little is known of the subject.

Focussing on a particular historical case of urban-industrial growth, Asa Briggs has offered

---

Regional Setting: A Scientific Survey, British Association for the Advancement of Science, Birmingham, 1950, 173; See, however, G. C.Allen, The Industrial Development of Birmingham and the Black Country, G. Allen and Unwin, London, 1929, 13-45, in which potable water supply is credited for the growth of the city. Transportation seems most important to C. Gill (History of Birmingham, Vol. I Manor and Borough to 1865, Oxford University Press, London, 1952, 87-8), although Gill, like W. C. Aitken ("Brass and Brass Manufactures," Birmingham and the Midlands Hardware District, S. Timmins, ed., Robert Hardwicke, London, 1866, reprinted by A. M. Kelley, N. Y., 1968, 227) and H. Hamilton (The English Brass and Copper Industries to 1800, Longmans, Green and Co., Ltd., London, 1926, 139) also stressed the availability of skilled labor.

[4] C. P. Kindleberger, Europe's Postwar Growth: The Role of Labor Supply, Harvard University Press, Cambridge, 1967; H. J. Habakkuk, American and British Technology in the Nineteenth Century; the Search for Labour-Saving Inventions, Cambridge University Press, 1967.

grist for further investigation and analysis.[5] Using suppositions about their respective labor forces, he drew sharp economic and social distinctions between Birmingham and Manchester.[6]

Manchester appeared as the archetypal new industrial city, with its vast mills and undifferentiated masses, plunging into the future with new technologies and markets. Harboring textile factories, whose workers inspired Marx and Engels to envision a reserve industrial army of the unemployed, Manchester developed a reputation as a smoke-clogged, dank, over-crowded, soul-killing maw for human life.

Despite its rapid increase in population and wealth, Birmingham remained essentially untouched by the new industrial era, Briggs argued. Unaffected by technological change, the city continued its pre-industrial specialization on hardwares like nails, tools, pots and pans, producing intermediate goods for industry and mundane necessaries for household life. As a result, skilled workers remained a higher percentage of the workforce than in Manchester and retained their high incomes.

---

[5] Asa Briggs, Victorian Cities, Penguin, Middlesex, 1968 and the more documented Odhams Press edition, 1963. Citations here apply to the revised later edition.

[6] Ibid., 186-7.

Because of its greater worth, education received more support in Birmingham than in Manchester.

Briggs contended that the variety of trades insulated Birmingham from severe economic fluctuation because workers could shift jobs easily, and the few technological changes that occurred complemented rather than replaced skilled labor. Thus, men did not fear competition from women and children, and because of high skill but low capital requirements, Birmingham workers had better chances for upward mobility than their Manchester counterparts. The pattern of growth in Birmingham resulted in continued predominance of workshops rather than factories. Because of those four characteristics - high skill component (which was the heart of the difference), neutral technological change, ease of mobility, and retention of the workshop system - Birmingham stood as a curious example of preindustrial survival in an industrial world.

Several theoretical and empirical questions surround Briggs' argument. First, abundance of trades need not preclude short-time work. Birmingham suffered national recessions as deeply as any other city in England during the industrial revolution, and the ability to shift employment from one industry to another was meaningful only if jobs were available in the second industry. Supply characteristics such as skill transferability are relevant to labor market analysis only within a context that includes a demand schedule for those skills. Thus the potential for inter- or even intra-industry job shifts might have been realized only infrequently in both short and long run. Also, despite the apparent diversity of output, most of Birmingham's unique trades fell under the umbrella of hardwares, among which guns, brass and jewellery were most prominent. Given the complementarity of such goods, a decline in one line of brasswares would just as likely bring a fall in similar lines.

Second, Briggs does not prove that Birmingham had relatively more skilled workers than Manchester, in part because he failed to define the term. Evidence from the Children's Employment Commission suggests that much Birmingham labor was semi-skilled and unskilled because job operations were relatively simple. A contemporary observor noted that the"great resemblance of many of the processes of work in different trades, or the small amount of skill and training required" encouraged quick entry into the gun trade, for example, at peak periods.[7] Wage evidence from the Board of Trade reports, for example, suggest that wages were, if anything, higher in the industrial north than in the midlands.[8]

---

7 Children's Employment Commission, Third Report of the Commission, 1864, 51.

8 Board of Trade, Returns of Wages Published between 1830 and 1886, 1887, passim.

Third, upward mobility is a tricky concept. Workers might feel upwardly mobile if they can own their own shops, but income does not always rise greatly with ownership. Also, as Lord noted, even in the 18th century, entering the hardware trade cost from £500 to £2000, no mean sum.[9]

Fourth, factories and workshops did not necessarily draw from different labor pools. Even well into the 19th century Mantoux's early 18th century factory, simply a collection of workers under one roof, often underwent little change.[10] Although often characterized as the hallmark of the skilled artisan, the workshop, with its large complement of women and children, seems to have required a rather smaller percentage of skilled workers than once thought. In any case, attention here falls not on output but on the types of labor demanded by the production process. Unskilled and semi-skilled labor, along with a fair proportion of skilled labor formed common labor pools for both factory and workshop. Persons with even minor talent for metal working seem to have been able to find jobs in almost any size or type of hardware establishment, for example.

---

[9] J. Lord, Capital and Steam Power 1750-1800, P. S. King and Son, London, 1923, 57-8.

[10] P. Mantoux, The Industrial Revolution in the 18th Century, Harper and Row, New York, 1961, Introduction; R. Church, Kenricks in Hardware: A Family Business: 1791-1966, David and Charles, Newton Abbot, 1969, 38, 55.

According to Briggs, Manchester and Birmingham attracted two different types of entrepreneurs and workers: to Manchester came employers with large capital sums and mastery of large-scale organization but employees with relatively few skills needed for simple production methods; to Birmingham came worker-entrepreneurs with modest sums but sharp senses of market vagaries and workers with heavy investment in skills. Manchester drew talented entrepreneurs; Birmingham drew talented workers who could easily become entrepreneurs.

In sum, ambiguity surrounding three characteristics of the labor force seem to underlie the confusion. One, as cited, there is no definition of skilled labor. Two, the proportion of skilled labor, however defined, in the labor force has not been measured. Three, relative incomes in Birmingham and Manchester also remain unmeasured. Until these problems are resolved, the approach toward understanding the alleged differences between the two urban labor forces remains impeded.

Aside from these definitional and empirical concerns, there seems to be a fundamental theoretical problem regarding the continued advantage of a large proportion of skilled workers receiving relatively higher wages than similar workers in another area. If wages were higher in Birmingham, one would expect a flow over time from Manchester to Birmingham, equalizing the wage differentials.

Undoubtedly, in absolute terms, a large proportion of the population can be skilled and have higher earnings relative to the nonskilled in the same area. It does not logically follow, however, that this skilled group would be relatively better off than a similar group in another area either initially or over time.

Thus the key to understanding the hypothesized economic difference between the two labor forces seems not only conditions on the supply side, as suggested by the stress on skills and proportions of skilled labor, but also conditions on the demand side. At its heart the traditional argument avers that high and sustained demand for skilled labor in Birmingham, resulting from the skill-intensive, workshop nature of the production process, resulted in higher wages over time in Birmingham than in Manchester. Such higher incomes would naturally have made skilled workers economically and socially more secure.

There are reasons to question such an interpretation, however. First, before and during the industrial revolution, Birmingham developed a highly specialized method of production. With work tasks thus fragmented, and made simpler, one would expect the demand for skilled labor in production to decline. Second, because of these simpler operations, Birmingham employed women and children to a great extent throughout the period, also suggesting a dampened demand for skilled labor.

Third, until definitional and empirical issues just discussed are resolved, one can make no firm analyses about any aspects of the labor force in Birmingham or Manchester. Thus, Birmingham might well have had more skilled workers proportionately, but they need not have been relatively better off. Thus, there might have been proportionately more skilled workers but they might have been relatively worse off. Conversely, Birmingham might have had relatively fewer skilled workers, but they might have been relatively better paid.

Briggs rightly argued that the nature of the labor force available to entrepreneurs helped determine the timing, pace, and nature of industrialization. Extending the thrust of his interpretation a bit, one might hypothesize that if Manchester could have obtained only expensive skilled labor, textile industries would not have "taken off" before the development of more productive, labor-displacing machinery. In Birmingham, hardware industries would have never adapted to changing markets because workers would not have had the capacity to do so.

Although intriguing, such propositions cannot yet be tested because they are not clearly counterfactual. So little is known of labor markets in Manchester and Birmingham that the"facts" are not securely enough established to be countered.

On close empirical investigation, therefore, the alleged differences between the two labor markets might evaporate. In any case, the key, overarching question throughout an analysis must ask how the demand for labor changed during the industrial revolution.

Unfortunately, economic historians have generally neglected Birmingham, despite its rapid growth and size during the industrial revolution. Three reasons seem responsible.

First, the most dramatic developments occurred in primary iron, coal, and textiles, of which Birmingham had virtually none, ceding leadership to the nearby Black Country and to the north. Several times entrepreneurs tried to set up textile mills in Birmingham but failed miserably.[11]

Birmingham did grow magnificently in secondary production, chiefly hardwares. Such industry lacked physical size and attention-gathering technological change, serving other industries by supplying items like screws, bolts, and edge tools. Thus, the hardware

---

11 Why Birmingham failed to develop in textiles remains unclear. Stanley Chapman argues that Birmingham textile works were not tightly linked to the Midland textile industry which, itself, failed to stimulate the engineering and machine building industries that gave the North a competitive edge. Why such linkages

industry has drawn little notice.

Second, throughout the turbulent years of the early 19th century, when other major centers like Manchester, Leeds, and Sheffield reeled from periodic social explosions, Birmingham workers remained fairly content, despite the enormous size of the city and the importance of industry. Class tensions seemed nowhere evident and no one really knows why. Indeed, in his massive volume on the English working class, E. P. Thompson makes scant reference to Birmingham, one of the largest industrial cities in the world.[12] Yet, although reportedly a location of great mobility for the hardworking artisan, the same families that occupied the highest political and commercial positions in 1800 occupied them in 1850. Scholars must incorporate Birmingham into discussions of social reaction to technological change or at least explain why they do not.

Third, doing research on a major industrial center characterized by small workshops that

---

failed to evolve still seems a murky area. S. Chapman, The Early Factory Masters: The Transition to the Factory System in the Midlands Textile Industry, David and Charles, Newton Abbot, 1967, 210, 213-14.

12 E. P. Thompson, The Making of the English Working Class, Gallancz, London, 1963.

left few if any records quickly induces frustration and a sense of chaos and hopelessness. Unlike the famous Strutt, Arkwright, and other massive textile archives of the Manchester area which continue to raise questions about business and industrial history, Birmingham has almost no accounts of industrial activity outside the unrepresentative Boulton and Watt collection, and only a few records of commercial enterprises. The city had hundreds of different types of industries with thousands of small firms, but only a few scraps of paper remain as testament. On questions at the firm or workshop level of fluctuations in daily employment, quantities of raw and semi-finished material purchased or sold, credit, and marketing arrangements, and adoption of new small-scale technologies, investigators find only a few scribblings on a stark blank wall. Only parts of the surrounding structure, like parliamentary reports and newspaper advertisements and comments, give some form to the edifice.

Considering the difficultly of creating order out of the welter of small metal industries, it is not surprising that only a few authors have tried to investigate the city at all. G.C. Allen and W.H.B. Court have written of Birmingham and Midland industries, but no one has considered Birmingham hardware industries as an integral part of the industrial revolution.[13] So overwhelming an image has Manchester posed that the industrial revolution is often defined in terms of the factory system, when in fact there was no necessary relation between the two.

Scholars must incorporate Birmingham and its hardware industries into the intellectual scaffolding used to view the industrial revolution. Birmingham industries made tools that built factories, guns that opened markets for an empire, and cheap household wares like pots and pans that eased the life of every household. Surely the city deserves better of economic historians. Birmingham industries participated fully in the industrial revolution, not as an aberration but as another aspect of a multi-faceted transformation that continues to raise more questions than it answers.

For years historians have lived with stereotypes about industrial change that have colored their perceptions of social and economic phenomena. Thus, the industrial revolution has come to be identified primarily with (and defined by) large scale factory production in textiles, iron, and coal with little appreciation of backward and

---

[13] G. C. Allen, Birmingham and the Black Country; W. H. B. Court, Rise of the Midland Industries, Oxford University Press, London, 1938.

forward linkages in other industries and even services, and with little credit to independent innovations like small but cumulative technological developments in small-scale manufacturing.

Birmingham workers and entrepreneurs helped create one of the most impressive industrial centers in the modern world. Scholars must now begin to ask more critically why they could do so.

To begin such an explanation, this study takes the following approach.

Chapter 2 briefly discusses the economic history of Birmingham, focussing on the diversity of output and changes in the economic structure of the city during the industrial revolution.

Chapter 3 investigates entrepreneurship and the related issue of mobility. The chapter asks how entrepreneurs in Birmingham differed from those in Manchester, if at all, and also investigates methods of financing industrial development and barriers to entry to see if mobility attracted workers to Birmingham as much as thought.

Chapter 4 asks specifically how labor fit into the industrialization experience unique to Birmingham, seeking to determine which qualities and quantities of labor were demanded and supplied over time and whether Birmingham labor markets differed from those in other major industrial centers.

Chapter 5 asks where Birmingham workers and entrepreneurs came from and what relative advantage they found in Birmingham, and whether Birmingham industries or the city itself invested heavily in training and education.

Chapter 6 seeks to identify changes in demands for services that might have influenced factor and product markets in Birmingham.

The final section offers conclusions that stress the complexity of industrial change and emphasize the need to re-assess Birmingham, with its relatively uninvestigated complex of industries, to broaden understanding of the industrial revolution.

CHAPTER TWO: ECONOMIC HISTORY OF BIRMINGHAM

Birmingham at the Beginning of the Industrial Revolution: 1777

Although most industries before the industrial revolution were highly labor intensive, unique factors made Birmingham trades more so. Several miles from Black Country iron and coal deposits, and facing high transportation costs before the canal age, 18th century Birmingham industries concentrated on assembly and finishing processes, which required much labor and for which costs of raw materials and transportation were low relative to total cost.

The nature of increased demand in the 18th century favored those industries in which Birmingham had long specialized - highly finished products like buckles, guns, brass, and copper ware,for example. For various reasons, including, according to one observor, a relative lack of water power, Birmingham devoted attention to manufactures, such as guns, which required little raw material (gun parts were made in towns nearer the iron and coal deposits and assembled in Birmingham) but much processing and some skill.[1] Despite the effort to produce quality goods, however, Birmingham was notorious for its "cheap toys", an image its manufacturers tried hard to dispel, with mixed success.[2]

Developments in the Black Country in semi-manufactures also benefited Birmingham.[3] Semi-finished gun locks and other parts made in Bilston, Wednesbury, and Darlaston and district were finished and assembled in Birmingham.[4] With developments like the stamp and press and more advanced casting techniques, Birmingham could work well with Black Country sheet metal.[5] Thus, even as the industrial revolution began to exert

---

[1] M. J. Wise, "Some Factors Influencing the Growth of Birmingham," Geography, vol. 33, 1948, 184; G. C. Allen, The Industrial Development of Birmingham and the Black Country, Allen and Unwin, London, 1929, 13-45.

[2] P. K. Dent, Old and New Birmingham, Houghton and Hammond, Birmingham, 1880, 111-113.

[3] G. C. Allen, The Industrial Development of Birmingham and the Black Country, 13-45.

[4] Wise, "Factors," 184.

[5] Allen, The Industrial Development of Birmingham and the Black Country, 13-45.

its influence on Birmingham, conflicting pressures on the labor market evolved: skilled labor was needed for at least some functions in assembly, while only unskilled and semi-skilled labor was cheap enough to bring advantage in finishing, stamping,and pressing.

With easier access to sources of raw material supplies and through improved transportation in the late 18th and early 19th century, Birmingham could shift from light metal "toys" to tubes, heavy castings, and steam engine components, which still required much labor.[6]

For centuries a relatively unimportant country town, Birmingham had surpassed Coventry, Warwick, Shrewsbury, and Worcester, which were historically well established industrial, commercial, or governmental centers in the West Midlands, by 1750. It was then only beginning to enter a phase of rapid growth that would triple Birmingham's population from 25,000 in 1750 to about 75,000 in 1800. At the beginning of the 18th century, Birmingham was fourth largest city in England and

---

[6] C. Gill, History of Birmingham , Vol. 1, Oxford University Press, 1952, 87-8. See also Henry Rees, "Birmingham and the Black Country," Economic Geography, 1946, 133-41. Note also the second volume of the History of Birmingham by Asa Briggs, *passim*.

Wales, far behind London but closely trailing Liverpool and Manchester.[7]

From the founding of the city's first brass works in 1740, Birmingham manufactures rapidly grew more industrially complex than its neighbors, although lacking sufficient profit and cost figures one cannot determine whether Birmingham benefited from high value added (resulting from a comparative advantage in skilled labor) or high volume (resulting from a comparative advantage in unskilled or semi-skilled labor). According to an early historian, the profitability of producing ornamental goods induced technological innovation and specialization of labor, attracting skilled workers and forcing less skilled (and less profitable) metal working operations into the countryside. Thus, simple smiths and nailmakers retreated to small Black Country towns like Walsall, Willenhall, Wednesbury, Dudley, and Stourbridge, while Birmingham advanced in buttons, jewellery, turnery, glass ware, and similar goods.[8] More broadly, Birmingham took the lead in producing

---

[7]R. K. Dent, The Making of Birmingham, Allday, London, 1894, 54. J. Jaffray, Hints for a History of Birmingham, Journal Office, Birmingham, 1857, Ch. 7, Census of England and Wales 1861.

[8]William Hawkes Smith, Birmingham and South Staffordshire, Charles Tilt, London, 1838, 18.

hardwares of all sorts and for the next several decades supplied world markets with work tools, household implements, guns, and brass articles and other items.[9] Because producing many of these newer goods demanded few skills because of new technologies, the overall impact on the labor market remains ambiguous.

Theoretically there are several ways to identify distinguishing characteristics of industries. One could investigate certain qualities by industry or firm such as assets, output, sales, profit, and employment. Unfortunately data remaining for 18th and 19th century Birmingham permit scant use of these indices. However, one could obtain at least a crude picture of the importance of certain industries for entrepreneurs by ranking the most numerous firms by type of activity, using qualitative data to add perspective. Such information would help rank economic areas by mobility because the most common trades would presumably allow easiest entry. The risk of error is high, of course, because a few firms might dominate an entire activity. Nonetheless, such an approach would offer the first glimpse at entrepreneurial structure and mobility in Birmingham.

By the beginning of the industrial revolution, metal trades like buttonmaking and plating

---

[9] Jaffray, Hints, Ch. 17.

unquestionably stood high in the structure of the Birmingham economy. A directory for 1777 supplied the data for identifying the most important activities, by numbers of firms or workshops.[10]

Type of Activity	# Firms		# Firms
Victuallers	248	Brass founders	46
Buttonmakers	129	Shopkeepers	39
Shoemakers	99	Bucklemakers	39
Merchants	77	Gunmakers	36
Tailors	74	Jewellers	35
Bakers	64	Maltsters	26
Toymakers	56	Drapers	24
Platers	52	Gardeners	23
Butchers	49	Plumbers & Glaziers	21
Carpenters	48		
Barbers	46	Ironmongers	21
		Total	1252

Although a large percentage of firms performed domestic and city-serving functions like shoemaking and construction, more unique industries

---

10 The Pearson and Rollason Directory, edited and rearranged by Charles Scarse,listed 286 different trades, covering 2297 establishments in 1777 when Birmingham's population was about 50,000. The directories are far from complete and are useful only to judge wide shifts in magnitude and trend. These 2297 firms probably did not include many very small operations that chose not to advertise either because their business was strictly local, or because they were already full-time subcontractees to much larger enterprises, like Boulton and Watt, or because they simply could not afford it. They did not indicate size of firm. Charles E. Scarse, ed. and compiler, <u>Birmingham 120 Years Ago,</u> Birmingham, 1896, a

like buttonmaking accounted for a strikingly high proportion of activity.

Several characteristics of the city's industrial activity stand out: First, much production focussed on special demands of exporters, especially those engaged in supplying buyers in such distant markets as America and West Africa.[11]

Second, nearly all important non-service trades involved metals. The directory cited no spinners, only one wool-comber, two flax-dressers, and three weavers. Thus, as the industrial revolution in textiles took hold in the North and even other Midland areas like Derbyshire and Nottinghamshire, Birmingham entrepreneurs

---

revised edition of The Birmingham Directory: or Merchant and Tradesmen. Useful Companion, Pearson and Rollason, Birmingham, 1777. For further discussion see Benjamin Walker, "Birmingham Directories," Birmingham Archaelogical Society Transactions, 1937, 1-36, and Jane E. Norton, Guide to the National and Provincial Directories of England and Wales, Excluding London, published before 1856, Royal Historical Society Guides and Handbooks No. 5, London, 1950, especially the introduction. The population estimate for 1777 appears in Showell's Directory of Birmingham, W. Showell and Sons, T. Harmon, compiler, Birmingham, 1885.

11 R. Pelham, "The West Midland Iron Industry and the American Market in the 18th Century", University of Birmingham Historical Journal, 1949-50, 141-62.

showed no interest, despite a good transportation system and proximity to the London market.[12]

Third, nonferrous metals had developed rapidly, although Birmingham brass manufacturers had started with major locational disadvantages. Except for fuel and fine casting sand used to make moulds, Birmingham had no raw materials nearby, for copper and calamine were both available only at a distance.[13] Birmingham did have workers skilled in preparing molds, fitting and finishing articles, and for the iron industry, the skills were perhaps transferable. [14]

Fourth, most trades were amenable to domestic or subcontracting work. The thirty-six gunmakers do not include those making only gun parts. Thus in 1777 there were also three gunlock masters, four gun finishers, six gun barrel makers,and two gun stock makers. Birmingham concentrated on processing, finishing and assembling parts made in the

---

12 For a full discussion of this phenomenon see Stanley D. Chapman, _The Early Factory Masters: The Transition to the Factory System in the Midlands Textile Industry_, David and Charles, Newton Abbot, 1967, 210-218.

13 W. C. Aitken, "Brass and Brass Manufacturers," _Birmingham and the Midland Hardware District_, S. Timmins, ed., 1866, reprinted by A. Kelley, New York, 1968, 225.

14 _Ibid._, 226.

South Staffordshire coal region in towns like Wednesbury.[15]

By the late 18th century, Birmingham had set up a strong industrial base which, however, lacked the impressive technological innovation and large scale of the textile, coal, and primary iron trades.

Thus, although the home of Watt's steam engine, Birmingham used rather few of them. Although the maker of household conveniences, Birmingham made none of the iron which spawned them. Although the creator of buttons, ornaments, and jewellery that enhanced Manchester textiles, Birmingham made none of the cloth. An unnoticed spinsterly sister, Birmingham undramatically minded its own business, which was the business of everyday life.

Birmingham during the Industrial Revolution: 1777-1830

Between 1777 and 1830, manufacturing in Birmingham changed considerably. Although workshop hardware industries remained important, new activities appeared and rankings of estab-

---

[15] M. J. Wise, "On the Evolution of the Jewellery and Gun Quarters in Birmingham," *Transactions of the Institute of British Geographers*, 1949, 65.

lished industries changed.[16]

Type of Activity: 1830	# Firms
Victuallers	509
Shopkeepers and dealers in groceries,etc.	244
Butchers	194
Academics	154
Jewellers, mfg.	152
Boot and shoe makers and whses.	143
Tailors and Drapers	143
Brass founders	132
Grocers and tea dealers	128
Platers and mfrs. of plated arts	122
Coal and coke merchants & dealers	113
Factors	101
Gun and pistol makers	101
Gilt toy makers	100
Merchants	92
Button makers	91
Plumbers, glaziers, painters	90
Builders	81
Maltsters	75
Cabinet makers, brokers, upholsterers	72
Surgeons	71
Steel toy makers, heavy and light	67
Total	2975

Although export trade expanded perhaps relatively slowly, home trade increased dramatically, especially in urban consumer goods, stimulating further specialization. Closely integrated to the large and growing national market, Birmingham trades found considerable profit at home. As income rose throughout

16 W. West, The History, Topography, and Directory of Birmingham, R. Wrightson, Birmingham,1830.

Britain, patterns of demand increasingly reflected the growth of the lower and middle income groups that provided stable markets for Birmingham products.

The trend toward specialization accelerated rapidly: For example, besides the 91 button makers there were 49 pearl button manufacturers and six button shank and cramp makers in 1830. Besides the 101 gun and pistol makers there were eight other types of firms, including 23 gun barrel makers, six gun stock makers, and 31 gun lock and furniture forgers and filers.

The entire Birmingham cabinet industry, dependent almost entirely on the home market, consisted of 19 cabinet makers in 1777, but by 1830 the industry had greatly specialized and increased to 8 cabinet and dressing case and portable dress makers and 72 cabinet makers, brokers and upholsterers. In 1777 there was one coach maker and one coach painter; in 1830 there were 20 coach builders, 27 coach furniture and harness platers, 9 coach harness and furniture makers, 5 coach lace fringe manufacturers, and 6 coach spring manufacturers. Thus, although production for export seems to have developed well enough within the basic industries, the growing consumer market seems to have stimulated much broader change in manufacturing.

The following trades also grew faster than population, which increased from 50,000 in 1777 to 144,000 in 1831.

Activity	1777	1830
Fender makers	2	31
Gilders	3	25
Metal rollers	3	17
Saddlers' ironmongers	1	16
Screw makers	2	16
Silversmiths	4	37
Snuff box maker	1	7
Snuffer makers	5	32
Spectacle makers	3	19
Spoon makers	1	30
Thimble makers	4	21
Tinplate workshops	5	24
Toolmakers*	10	50
Wheelwrights	4	26
Coopers	9	41
Chairmakers	1	13
Casters	9	35

*Edge tool makers explicitly included for 1830, and probably, though not explicitly, included in 1777.

By 1830 then, metal working remained vital to Birmingham and in response to wider and deeper markets had specialized appropriately. Entrepreneurs and workers found gain in spinning off from established lines to produce allied goods. The affect of this process on either entrepreneurs or workers remains unclear, however. Specialization tends to reduce the number of skills and amount of judgement a worker must have. One would expect a general lowering of skill requirements in industries rapidly engaging in specializing. Such a process might have a reverse effect on entrepreneurs, reducing costs, allowing easier entry and expansion.

In this 50 year period, Birmingham industries responded quickly to changes in demand but seemingly found little reason to alter the nature of the labor supply. Newly important industries like cabinet and coach making did not require new production techniques, but continued to demand much the same type of employee as needed in the pre-industrial context.

Such structural stability during the turbulent years of the industrial revolution seems remarkable for a major industrial city. Periods of sharp national depression came in 1800, 1810, 1812, 1817, 1819, and 1830.[17] By the end of the Napoleonic Wars, Birmingham trade with the United States, its biggest overseas customer, declined largely because the Americans were beginning to produce their own goods. Birmingham merchants and manufacturers thus pushed for the Far Eastern trade, but exports in general failed to remain as important to Birmingham in the 1815-40 period

---

17 Jaffray, Hints, Ch. 44.

as before.[18]

With the maturity of Birmingham as a business center, the city's entrepreneurs responded to changing problems and conditions in other ways. Although they faced a wide range of economic problems, the two hundred businesses that formed the Birmingham Chamber of Commerce focussed on a few problems and pursued solutions for them through Parliamentary lobbying activities. Using precedent set only by Leeds, Halifax, and Exeter, Birmingham businessmen set up the Chamber in 1783.[19] Relatively quiet for the first few years, the Committee mainly pressed for lower taxes, prohibition of tool exports (to potential Continental and American competitors), and greater access to a steady, cheap supply of brass and copper. A chief concern was to maintain

---

18 D. E. C. Eversley, "Industry and Trade of 1500-1800," Victoria History of the Counties of England - A History of the County of Warwick, W. B. Stevens, ed., Vol. VII, The City of Birmingham, Oxford University Press, 1964, 118.

19 G. Henry Wright, Chronicles of the Birmingham Chamber of Commerce A. D. 1813-1913 and of the Birmingham Commercial Society A. D. 1783-1812, Birmingham, 1913, 11.

a stable labor force and it concentrated on efforts to stem the flow abroad of Birmingham manufacturers and workmen.[20] Like most commercial societies set up during the Napoleonic Wars, however, the Birmingham group did little publicly or at least published little.[21]

Renewed and renamed in 1813 with about 200 members paying a guinea a year, the Chamber of Manufacturers and Commerce early joined to campaign to repeal the Corn Laws, which, it complained, forced employers to pay artifically high wages. In the same year the Chamber made the first of several recommendations to readjust the labor market, arguing for drastic changes in the Elizabethan Statute of Artificers to eliminate seven year apprenticeships.[22]

In 1816 the Chamber focussed nearly all its efforts against Peel's bills to regulate and inspect all factories employing 20 or more people under 18 years of age and attacked a similar measure in 1818.[23]

---

[20] Ibid., 15-21.

[21] Ibid., 48.

[22] Ibid., 602.

[23] Ibid., 70-2, 72.

Birmingham business not only sought periodically to loosen the labor market by eliminating training restrictions, but also tried to strengthen its strong position in the world metal goods trade by restricting emigration of artisans and export of machinery.[24]

Unfortunately, records from 1830 to the mid-1850s are barren, providing no indication of how Birmingham business reacted to the new trade union movement nationally or locally. As Chapter Four observes, newspapers and other sources suggest that Birmingham entrepreneurs, unlike their counterparts in other industrial cities, felt compelled to devote little attention to problems of organized labor. Even by the mid-19th century city businessmen boasted of their control over labor, even while the Chartists frightened London and the Luddites the North.[25]

Birmingham after the Industrial Revolution: 1830-1860

Birmingham quickly adapted to the demands

---

24 *Ibid*., 77, 88, 89.

25 W. Ryland, "The Plated Wares", S. Timmins, ed., *Birmingham and the Midlands Hardware District*, 1866, A. Kelley, New York, 1968, 479.

of the nascent engineering age. Although traditional Birmingham trades, like brass-making and jewellery, continued to thrive and retain their lead in numbers of establishments from 1830 to 1860, some staples, like "toys", declined relatively, but new industries appeared. Not surprisingly, the new trades relied heavily on the city's long experience in metal working.

But heavier trades like electroplating, bedsteads, railroad rolling stock, sewing machines, and machinery grew rapidly.[26] Equally notable was the growth of production of ship sheathing, which rose from a negligible industry in 1830 to one employing 500 men and boys and producing 100 tons of sheathing a week in 1863.

Birmingham and vicinity consumed ten times more copper for sheathing, tubing, casting, wire and other trades in 1863 than in the 1830s, forging deep linkages with suppliers.[27]

Feeding into the latest technologies,

---

26 Eversley, "Industry and Trade", 125.

27 J. Skirrow Wright, "An Account of some New Trades in Birmingham, and Phases of its Social Life since 1832," Transactions of the National Association for the Promotion of Social Science, 1863, 826.

entrepreneurs began after 1840 producing brass tubing for locomotive and marine boilers, and by mid-century railway carriage-making employed about a thousand people in three or four big firms.[28] Work in the metallic bedstead industry grew from only four firms in the mid-1840s to 50 in 1863.

Birmingham also grew in making steel pens, with over 2000 workers (80 percent of them women and girls) in the 1860s. The few skilled men were mainly tool-makers.[29]

Always important to Birmingham, jewellery making felt a sharp boost from the greater availability and cheapness of gold after the California strikes in the 1850's. Birmingham manufacturers processed 3000 ounces of gold and 6000 ounces of silver a week, exclusive of that used in gilding and plating and making forks, spoons, services of silver plate. Between 1832 and 1863 the number of jewellery masters grew from 20 to 250 and the number of employees from 200 to 3000, plus those in subsidiary occupations like lapidaries, die-sinkers, enamellers, and case makers.

Other relatively new, prospering trades included hooks and eyes, photographic equipment

---

28 Ibid., 826-827.

29 Ibid., 827.

and electroplating.[30] The attractiveness of the city to such new activities suggests many characteristics: external economies, existence of a large market, factors of production attuned to metalworking. Clearly labor loomed as but a single consideration among many facing entrepreneurs. Yet in many respects it stood most important, for a restive workforce of talented persons could abort an operation easily. Thus, the less irreplaceable and the more acquiescent the labor pool, the greater advantage held by the city in attracting investing residents.

Before assessing the impact of this new industrial sector on the labor force, it is necessary to understand more comprehensively precisely what changes occurred. By number of firms the top industrial trades seem to have shifted position hardly at all even as late as 1860, according to data from a directory for that year.[31]

---

30 *Ibid*., 827-8.

31 *Post Office Directory of Birmingham*, Kelley and Co., London, 1860.

Type of Activity: 1860	# Firms
Shopkeepers	1207
Beer retailers	1029
Public houses, inc. Hotels, Inns, Taverns	763
Grocers and Tea Dealers	446
Tailors	378
Bakers	328
Fruiterers & Greengrocers	320
Jewellers	319
Milliners & dressmakers	293
Schools	247
Buttonmakers	230
Plumbers, painters, glaziers	228
Coal dealers	224
Farmers	220
Draper	219
Butchers	194
Builders	175
Tobacconists	173
Brassfounders	171
Hairdressers	169
	7333

Among industries jewellers, buttonmakers, coal dealers, and brassfounders were predominant, betraying only slight difference from rankings in 1777 and 1830. Thus, new entrepreneurs went into generally traditional lines, suggesting perhaps that old activities offered more opportunity for mobility than the new.

Viewed in another perspective, however, much had changed, as shown in the following table:

Year	# Types of Firms	Annual % Change
1777	286	
		0.45
1830	355	
		5.0
1860	953	

Year	# of Firms	Annual % Change
1777	2,300	
		4.4
1830	7,700	
		5.3
1860	20,000	

Year	Population	Annual % Change
1777	50,000	
		3.6
1830	144,000	
		3.5
1860	296,000	

During the industrial revolution the number of Birmingham people and firms mushroomed. Population grew 3.6 percent a year (simple rate) and the number of firms 4.4 percent. The variety of firms, however, changed by less than one-half percent a year. Thus, as the city exploded in size, most of its producers supplied increasing amounts of roughly the same goods. Only a fairly narrow base generated employment and entrepreneurial opportunities.

By 1860, the situation had changed dramatically. Population growth slowed marginally although the number of firms increased somewhat more rapidly, but the most impressive difference occurred in the variety of firms which changed ten times faster after the industrial revolution than during it. Thus, employment and entrepreneurial opportunity surged ahead into a far wider network of activity by mid-century. Among the top 20 activities, services, including, for example, grocers and tea dealers, tailors, fruiterers and greengrocers, and milliners and dressmakers, grew rapidly, although industry changed relatively little.

Thus, during the industrial revolution, Birmingham underwent several major changes. The city became an industrial and commercial town of the first rank, serving regional, national, and international markets. Its industrial structure developed from a somewhat narrow hardware and toy producing sector into a complex and interconnected cluster of activities producing and serving a great variety of consumer and producer goods. Its entrepreneurs formed important pressure groups, especially before Parliament. Closely tied to the fortunes of the national economy, Birmingham fed a well-developed export and world trade. Yet it lacked large scale enterprises, such as the relatively giant textile mills of Lancashire, and the capital intensive features rightly or wrongly associated with the industrial revolution.

Several critical questions emanate from this pattern, and will be the main concern of the rest of this study. Did the new industries and services develop in Birmingham because of the existing supply of entrepreneurs and employees or did they change that supply? Did the opening of new entrepreneurial and employment opportunities attract persons with different skills or different degrees of old skills? Did the new activities change the comparative advantage Briggs felt Birmingham had in the skilled labor supply? Did the decidedly greater increase in specialization result in more or fewer skilled workers or did the extant quality and quantity encourage such specialization? More broadly, how did the timing, pace, and nature of industrialization affect the labor market in Birmingham? Available evidence suggests tentative but significant answers to these questions and new approaches for further inquiry.

CHAPTER THREE: BIRMINGHAM ENTREPRENEURS AND THE INDUSTRIALIZING EXPERIENCE

Whether or not economic and social mobility actually characterized the labor force in Birmingham, both contemporaries and later historians, such as Briggs, believed that it did. In distilled form the argument asserts that low fixed capital requirements allowed skilled workers to become masters with a modicum of savings. With their skills the most precious factor in the production process, such men needed only the opportunity to acquire a few implements and a modest shop to become entrepreneurs in their own right. Based on these assumptions - that entry costs were low and that low entry costs eased mobility - the traditional explanation stresses the uniqueness of Birmingham in remaining so "fluid" (undefined) while high capital costs and organizational rigidity ossified industrial society throughout the rest of Great Britain, particularly in Manchester.

When we submit the standard version to closer scrutiny, crucial empirical and theoretical questions arise. The major theoretical problem, around which several others revolve, lies in the apparent confusion between marginal and average conditions. What characterized some members of the labor force need not have affected all members. One cannot extrapolate from the mobility of a few in Birmingham (even if relatively more than in Manchester) to the mobility of the many. By focussing on the successes of some talented workshop owners who rose to entrepreneurial prominence, historians may well have described a path travelled by only a few.

Related empirical issues turn on this point. First, little evidence suggests that entry costs were uniformly "low", however defined. Historians have done so little empirical work on Birmingham firms that generalizations about business development are hazardous. Fixed capital setting up costs varied widely, even among hardware trades, and within specific trades capital sizes of the largest and smallest firms often differed substantially.

Second, costs of setting up might not have provided as serious a barrier to entry as costs of operation. Stressing entry costs might mislead attention from a different set of problems, those of acquiring short-term capital. Although the traditional picture of the textile industry emphasizes high fixed costs, at least one scholar had argued that variable costs played by far the more important role.[1] Increasingly others have

---

[1] Stanley D. Chapman, "Fixed Capital Formation in the British Cotton Industry, 1770-1815," Economic History Review, August 1970, 252. Lack of working capital constantly worried Birmingham entrepreneurs, for although suppliers often granted credit readily, workmen in the area would not wait and acted against payment in truck. Aris Birmingham Gazette, Jan. 18, 1830, Jan. 25, 1830.

also begun questioning the importance of fixed capital in different contexts. Livesay and Porter maintain that in the ante-bellum United States, working costs, especially wages, in industries like iron, textiles, and railway supply were by far the industrialist's greatest concern.[2] For example, in 1860 the E. I. du Pont powder company had a half million dollars invested in fixed capital assets, but spent 88 percent as much that year in operating costs.[3] Also in 1860 the Baldwin railway supply company had $350,000 in fixed capital assets but produced $750,000 worth of products. Wages consumed $251,000, fully 70 percent of the value of the firm's fixed capital assets.[4]

More important than percentages was the role of nonmanufacturers in handling intermediary financial arrangements, like discounting notes and lending on accounts receivable, which banks, insurance companies, and other traditional capital sources generally refused to do.[5] Those performing these merchanting

---

[2]H. Livesay, G. Porter, "The Financial Role of Merchants in the Development of U.S.Manufacturing, 1815-1860," _Explorations in Economic History_, Fall 1971, 63-87.

[3]_Ibid_., 75.

[4]_Ibid_., 76.

[5]_Ibid_., 78.

functions had considerable power over manufacturers. Benjamin Jones found it difficult to get credit for his iron works until James Laughlin, a merchant and bank stockholder, entered the firm as a partner and used his connections for the Jones and Laughlin Company.[6]

Although Livesay and Porter note differences between British and American banking communities, the basic economic situation seemed similar. Relatively new in such rapidly growing proportions, manufacturing quieted chary investors and creditors only after several decades'exposure. The relation to circumstances in Birmingham and Manchester seem plain in rough outline if not in detail. Unfortunately, the thrust is more negative than positive. Thus, it seems less clear that fixed costs in either city were prohibitively high for most artisans, if only because variable costs seem to have been even higher. Neither is it clear that obtaining credit was easier for Birmingham workshops than for Manchester factories because, if the United States case offers any insight, creditors scrutinized borrowers carefully, selecting, naturally, the most risk free and profitable. The situations in Britain and the United States or in Birmingham and Manchester might well have differed completely from this conjecture. The main point for the moment is that we simply do not know completely what the actual circumstances were and therefore must tread cautiously in our hypotheses. In any case, the

---

[6] Ibid., 64, 75.

propensity for greater mobility in one city over another, based on availability of credit for business expansion, seems only an assumption rather than an observation. Differences in capital size and structure between Birmingham hardwares and Manchester textiles might, therefore, also be illusory.

A third criticism of the conventional image follows a comment by a student of Midlands industrial history who recently noted that sources of capital in that area remain only incompletely known, for most attention has focussed on textile, coal, and iron industries.[7] How and where entrepreneurs get their funds, or whether obtaining funds was itself a major problem, has not received much investigation.

Fourth, even assuming that entrepreneurs and aspiring workers faced low entry costs and ready capital, what was mobility worth? Would not easy entry have led to surpluses of small entrepreneurs, depreciating the value of mobility? More precisely, what were the opportunity costs of remaining a worker? It is not at all clear that skilled workers, a scarce group everywhere in Great Britain, faced more serious disabilities in Manchester than in Birmingham.

---

[7] W. H. B. Court, reviewing S. Timmins, ed., Birmingham and the Midlands Hardware District, 1866, Economic History Review, April, 1969, 169.

To understand the dimensions and value of mobility in Birmingham vis-a-vis other industrial centers one must know whether Birmingham entrepreneurs actually faced different capital requirements and tapped more favorable capital markets.

Sources and Costs of Capital

The role of religious minorities in accumulating capital during the industrial revolution has justifiably received much comment. The ill-formed nature of 18th century business operations, with great risks, weak institutions, poor transportation and communication, slow legal redress, and lack of limited liability, put a premium on informal bonds like kinship.[8] For example, Quaker families in 1800 were quite prominent in such diverse fields as grain merchanting, milling, brewing, iron making and merchanting, and banking. Nonconformists generally shied away from activities like agriculture and mining, because they were so closely tied to landowning, the preserve of those of the established religion.[9] The financial strength of such groups deserves much attention: of the

---

[8] Peter Mathias, The First Industrial Nation, Methuen and Co., London, 1969, 161, 162.

[9] Ibid., 158.

£110,000 paid Henry Thale for his brewery in 1781 by Robert Barclay, Sylvanus Bevan, and John Perkins, £70,000 was lent by fellow Quakers.[10]

A refuge for Nonconformists since the 17th century, Birmingham offers ample illustration of the same pattern of financial dealings and aid. Quaker Richard T. Cadbury, born in 1768 in Exeter, apprenticed in Kent and Gloucester, employed by a silk mercer and draper in London, eventually moved to Birmingham in 1794 where he met Charles Lloyd and other Friends and opened a shop as a linen draper and silk mercer.[11]

Many other Birmingham entrepreneurs seem often to have garnered initial capital from informal sources. Thus, Archibald Kenrick, son of a prosperous small estate owner, quickly made contacts with influential fellow Unitarians

---

[10] Ibid., 160.

[11] W. A. Cadbury, Richard Tapper Cadbury, 1768-1860, privately printed, Birmingham, 1944, 5,6,7,8. Presumably, the Quaker community provided Cadbury with technical and financial aid. His two sons (one of whom inherited and later sold his shop eventually accumulated enough in chocolate making in Birmingham that one of the grandchildren could donate £170,000 worth of land and houses to a trust for workers' housing in 1900). Iola A. Williams, The Firm of Cadbury 1831-1931, Constable and Co., London, 1931, 4-5, 220. Richard himself long remained influential in Birmingham affairs, serving on the powerful Street Commission from 1801 to 1851 and acting as its chairman from 1836 to 1851. Cadbury, Richard Tapper Cadbury, 10-11.

shortly after arriving in Birmingham about 1780.[12] After receiving a small sum from his father, deducted from his inheritance, he assured himself of some financial security upon marriage in 1790 with a dowry of £500 and £500 annuity for his wife from her father.[13] From 1813 to 1851 retained earnings in his hardware firm provided the most important source of capital, although he resorted to trade credit, bank overdrafts and family loans occasionally. The dowry gave him a sound start in business, however.[14]

Of course, entrepreneurs in general desired varying amounts of capital for varying lengths of time and drew on several sources, including banks, saving clubs, inheritances, dowries, private and public loans, partnerships, retained earnings, and trade credit.

Although their precise contribution remains unmeasured, country banks provided capital and financial services and grew rapidly during much of the industrial revolution.[15] Such institutions

---

12 Roy A. Church, Kenricks in Hardware: A Family Business 1791-1966, David and Charles, Newton Abbot, 1969, 20.

13 Ibid., 23, 30.

14 Ibid., 46.

15 L. S. Pressnell, Country Banking in the Industrial Revolution, Oxford University Press, London, 1956, 7.

developed throughout the nation, the Birmingham area fostering more than its share. By 1800 the West Midlands had a lower ratio of population to bank offices than any other region in the country, including London.[16]

No single reason explains why the West Midlands required a relatively greater number and presumably a greater variety of financial services than London, or even the Manchester cotton trade region. Indeed, bank credit probably supplied less capital than trade credit or commercial paper. Pressnell noted that bills of exchange circulated at least as widely as bank notes and that banks rarely financed individuals trying to set up on small scale.[17] Some tradesmen practiced a lucrative trade in discounting bills, suggesting healthy demand for capital although of indeterminate size.[18]

In the Birmingham area, finance increasingly diverted resident entrepreneurs from industry. For example, Samuel Galton began working in the family gun firm in 1777, but ceased gunmaking in 1804 to start banking with his son and another

---

16 R. Cameron, ed., Banking in the Early Stages of Industrialization, Oxford University Press, New York, 1967, 26.

17 Pressnell, 246, 328.

18 *Ibid.*, 320.

man, and eventually handled much of the financial servicing for the gun trade.[19]

The city also attracted financial institutions from outside the region but seemed tardy in developing its own. The Bank of England opened a branch in 1827, but the Birmingham Banking Company, the first joint stock bank in Birmingham, did not appear until 1829.[20] Reflecting the lucrative market, the Bank declared a ten percent dividend, based on a twenty percent return on capital, in its first report.[21]

There is still little information on bank users, but it seems clear that those in 18th century Birmingham came from all types of occupations. Ten years after its founding in 1765, Lloyd's bank in Birmingham served such persons as a file-cutter, hinge-maker, barber, victualler,

---

19 Barbara M . D. Smith, "The Galtons of Birmingham: Quaker Gun Merchants and Bankers, 1702-1831," Business History, July 1967, 132-150.

20 W. F. Crick, J. E. Wadsworth, A Hundred Years of Joint Stock Banking, Holder and Stoughton, London, 1936, 53. As joint stock banks grew more popular, private banks declined, from six banking partnerships in 1829 to only three ten years later. The number of joint stock banks in Birmingham grew from one to seven during the same period. Ibid., 61-2.

21 Bank of Birmingham Report 1833, 4. Birmingham Reference Library.

butcher, and toymaker, most of whom were probably small tradesmen rather than employees.[22]

It is not clear, however, to which level of income banks most often reached. In 1838, for example, the average depositor in the Birmingham Savings Bank had £17.17s. in his account, which a contemporary deemed "much less than in other large towns."[23] Based apparently on relatively small deposits, the Bank grew considerably during the first half of the 19th century, as the following suggests.

Year	Number of Accounts	(£) Amount invested in Bank of England[24]
1830	2,600	48,000
1844	13,200	250,000
1850	19,800	347,000

By 1850, accounts greater than £100 formed only three percent of all depositors, but over one

---

22 R. S. Sayers, Lloyds Bank in the History of English Banking, Oxford, 1957, 89.

23 "Contributions to the Economical Statistics of Birmingham," Journal of the Statistical Society, 1839, 435.

24 Aris, January 25, 1830, November 25, 1844, and June 3, 1850.

quarter of all deposits.[25]

One must not overlook building and land societies, which grew from one to forty-two between 1842 and 1862, by which time over 25,000 depositors had subscribed about £2,250,000.[26] Members generally purchased shares in £120 units, investing 5s. every two weeks and receiving five percent interest. Within twelve to fourteen years shares were paid off. Members could also borrow, though solely to pay for a mortgage, at slightly over five percent.[27] There are no indications that such institutions performed functions similar to trade credit, but rather served as long run investing and borrowing mechanisms for individuals.

Nonbank institutions for saving and borrowing, like savings clubs in taverns, also flourished. These "money societies" took many forms and provided a mechanism for widespread accumulation of relatively small capital sums. Members made payments regularly, often every two weeks, and received interest on their contributions.[28] These

---

[25] Ibid., June 3, 1850.

[26] G. S. Johnson, "On the Benefit Building and Freehold Land Societies of Birmingham," Journal of the Royal Statistical Society, 1865, 517.

[27] Ibid., 511, 512.

[28] Aris, November 5, 1838.

clubs seemed to service a great variety of customers. For example, pubs often had savings clubs of £25, £50, and £100. Payments, especially for the latter (£1 every two weeks), clearly exceeded the means of most workingmen, who probably funnelled their money into friendly societies.[29] One can surmise several reasons for the popularity of such clubs. Workingmen probably used the smaller clubs (under £25) to secure themselves against the frequent and unpredictable downturns in trade. "Little Masters" probably found the larger clubs a convenient way to save for expansion or debt payment, especially, because deposits earned interest. Others, perhaps professionals or well-established tradesmen, might have used clubs more for personal purposes, to furnish a home or to finance travel or a son's education, for example. Established mainly in convenient social gathering places, the money societies offered a characteristically Victorian (or pre-Victorian) institutional mechanism for thrift. Although useful for individuals money societies were ill-suited for short-term lending.[30]

A more common method of increasing an enterprises's capital resources, rather than relying on financial intermediaries, was finding a partner. Entrepreneurs frequently took on partners to increase scale of operations, enter new operations

---

29 Birmingham Journal, March 10, 1860.

30 Ibid.

or fields, or penetrate mew markets. As business operations, partnerships had many advantages. They often encouraged specialization within the firm, with one partner handling production and the other distribution or marketing, for example. They enabled experienced journeymen to enter entrepreneurial ranks with little or no capital, and provided profitable outlets for investors seeking only to place funds rather than to manage operations. Conversely, they often allowed established manufacturers to acquire capital without sacrificing management control. Because limited liability laws were not passed until after the industrial revolution, the partnership form had a long while to germinate and develop laws and customs of its own. Common throughout England, it seemed especially suited to the small workshop environment of Birmingham, not necessarily for increased capacity, for manufacturers often worked separate premises even after partnerships, but for security over trade fluctuations and efficiencies in using scarce labor and management talent.

Unfortunately, few Birmingham partnership documents exist. The largest collection spans the late 18th and early 19th centuries, and when supplemented with other documents, provides a glimpse at sources and sizes of capital in some enterprises.[31]

---

[31] Lee, Crowder Collection, Partnership Deeds of Birmingham Firms 1783-1825, and West Hagley Deposit, Partnership Indentures, Box 258, Birmingham Reference Library.

Partnerships offered entrepreneurs opportunities to expand in allied trades. For example, William Lort, a Birmingham manufacturer who made steel trusses, surgical instruments, artificial limbs, glaziers, vices and moulds took on William Bragg, also a Birmingham truss maker, as a partner in 1825. Lort had over £600 worth of stock in trade, fixtures, tools, and implements. Bragg gave him about £300 and subsequently both shared costs and returns.[32]

About the same time Edward Biggs of Birmingham sought to expand his business as a wire drawer, metal roller, and manufacturer of metallic goods and wares, and, lacking capital himself, agreed to join with William Lee, a gentleman living near Birmingham, for 21 years. Biggs provided his physical capital plus funds to make his entire contribution £1000, while Lee supplied £2000.[33]

The firm of Crompton and Blyth also took a silent partnership form. Crompton, a gentleman residing in nearby Edgbaston, advanced £4000 to Blyth, a Birmingham merchant, factor, and commission agent. Crompton agreed to devote as much time and attention to the firm "as the nature of his other engagements will allow," but Blyth "shall and will without any extra allowance

---

32 Lee, Crowder Collection, Partnership Deeds of Birmingham Firms 1783-1825, March 21, 1825.

33 Ibid., October 26, 1822.

therefore devote himself wholly and exclusively to the said Copartnership concerns and apply his undivided attention and exertions for the sole benefit and advancement thereof."[34]

Working businessmen often invested in other firms without diverting attention from their own enterprises and silent partners were not always landed or independently wealthy persons or even merchants. During the Napoleonic Wars, Messrs. Dunderdale, Mabson, and Labron, Birmingham gunmakers and factors, combined at first unofficially and within 18 months formally for the typical 21 year partnership. Dunderdale and Mabson agreed to advance equal shares of money and stock in trade for a total of £15,000, charging no interest.[35] Dunderdale and Mabson would divide all capital and five-sixths of the profits, while Labron took the remaining one-sixth, probably because it appears that Labron was the only one who would actually work in the firm. Labron would attain full partnership, entitled to one-third of the profits and one-third share in all else, if he brought £5000 into the trade after five years. (Dunderdale and Mabson could then withdraw £2500 each, leaving the firm with £15,000 in capital.) Mabson and

---

34 Ibid., September 20, 1833.

35 Sidney Pollard has noted that drawing interest on invested capital was common in partnerships. The Genesis of Modern Management, Penguin Books, Middlesex, 1965, 272.

Dunderdale could, before Labron joined, continue their interests in several Birmingham public joint stock companies, although they could not engage in competing enterprises.[36]

Partners did not always have to present cash at the time of signing. For example, the merchanting firm of Stokes and Hunt, set up November 1, 1809 retroactive to July 1,1808, was founded with a capital value of £5000: Stokes provided £3000 and Hunt £2000, and each drew five percent interest yearly. Only with mutual consent could fixed capital expand. However, Hunt received only one-fifth the profits until he added £1000 beyond the original £2000, when he would earn one-fourth. The contract does not explain the disparity between the proportion of the contribution and the proportion of the return, but perhaps Hunt owed Stokes money or Stokes agreed to work unpaid while Hunt remained merely a passive investor. Both men, however, could apprentice one or more sons.[37]

Working manufacturers occasionally supplied funds to firms in the same trade, solely for a fixed return with no management responsibilities. For example, John Armitage, a Birmingham chemist

---

36 Closely paraphrased. Agreement settled June 23, 1808, retroactive to December 23, 1806. Lee, Crowder Collection, Partnership Deeds.

37 Lee, Crowder Collection, Partnership Deeds, November 1, 1809.

and refiner, agreed to take on as a partner John Clarke, a Birmingham chemist and druggist, in the chemist and refining business. Clarke contributed £3000, and Armitage provided buildings, money, stock, credits, and effects roughly equal to £3000. Exempt from work, Clarke got a guaranteed 15 percent return annually, while Armitage ran the business and got the rest. Clarke could also continue in his own right as a practicing chemist.[38]

Contract stipulations for partnerships varied widely in length of time, contributions and rates of return among partners, and total sizes of capital involved, making generalization difficult.

Occasionally, groups set up partnerships as adjuncts to going concerns, and even men in unrelated trades joined in partnerships to spread risks. For example, in 1814 John Simmons, John Parkes, and John Simmons Green, all Birmingham merchants, each contributed £700 to trade with Ireland. Parkes, obviously the junior partner and probably not long past a merchant apprenticeship, agreed to manage the firm for £80 the first year, £90 the second, and £100 the third and each succeeding year. Playing no active roles, Simmons and Green had access to all buildings and books, letters, bills, etc. Notably, the capital size was virtually unlimited, for whoever could provide extra capital would earn interest and an increased share of the profits. No partner could withdraw interest or capital for two years from the beginning

---

38 Ibid., September 29, 1814.

of the partnership.[39]

Mixed partnerships also occurred. Thus, in 1839 Henry Savage, an edge tool manufacturer, and Walter Allcock, a maltster, both near Birmingham, bought the trade of Samuel Savage, an edge tool manufacturer, and formed a 21 year partnership.[40]

Thus, banks, savings clubs, and partnerships all played an important if indeterminate role in local financing, but capital also came from other sources. Through several other channels,funds flowed into the city or were shifted within it, as reflected in newspaper advertisements placed by both investors and seekers of funds. Like partnerships, amounts and conditions of transfer took a welter of different forms. Publicly placed ads competed with banks and often with partnerships by offering or demanding roughly the same interest rate. Savings clubs generally paid depositors about half what they could get in the open market, which probably explains the small size of the clubs. With public offerings, the Birmingham capital market opened up to outsiders and prompted the growth of financial services,

---

[39] Ibid., February 15, 1814.

[40] West Hagley Papers, Partnerships Agreements, Box 259, Birmingham Reference Library, September 5, 1839. See also the Evans, Gibbs, and Canning partnership combining several lines of work to form an enterprise as coal masters, buck and pipe makers. West Hagley Collection, Partnership Indentures, Box 258, January 1, 1849.

especially through attorneys acting as intermediaries.[41]

The range of amounts of capital offered publicly ranged widely. Some offerings seem remarkably large for a city with an economy reputedly made up primarily of workshops, but their frequency suggests their widespread use.

Although advertisements appeared in such great numbers and in so many forms that precise classification is not feasible, some patterns emerge. Bypassing banks, stewards of trust funds offered money with perhaps greater frequency than any other single source, specifying exact sums and interest desired. Partners seeking investors and investors seeking silent or active partners also advertised often. With neither trust funds nor partnerships did discernible patterns develop over the years, however. Demands for capital in individual firms did not systematically rise or fall.

---

[41] B. L. Anderson has found the use of attorneys in such a role quite common in the North. "The Attorney and the Early Capital Market in Lancashire," J. R. Harris, ed., Liverpool and Merseyside Essays in the Economic and Social History of the Port and Its Hinterlands. Frank Cass and Co., 1969, 50-77.

Solicitors seem to have had varied duties in handling funds, including borrowing,lending and carrying out investors' wishes on security arrangements, offering money in many ranges, from a few hundred to several thousand pounds. Aris, April 16, 1832, April 7, 1834, April 14, 1834, January 15, 1838.

Indeed, the amounts of capital demanded and supplied seemed to belie the small workshop image of the city. Even in the early part of the century, entrepreneurs seeking funds for expansion asked for thousands rather than hundreds of pounds.[42] At the same time investors seeking active or passive roles in management expressed interest in placing thousands of pounds in manufacturing firms.[43] Reflecting the sophistication of the capital market, insouciant investors sought sleeping partnerships, unmindful what type of activity enterprises undertook.[44]

There was, therefore, a lively investment market in Birmingham, which transferred large sums as a matter of course. Investors and lenders offered tens of thousands of pounds in single transactions.[45] As insurance companies and other new institutions of capital accumulation developed, the market saw even more infusions of large sums.[46] In line with national interest charges, rates fluctuated

---

42 Aris, November 24, 1800, June 15, 1812, September 28, 1812.

43 Aris, May 7, 1810, May 14, 1810, February 9, 1801.

44 Ibid., October 7, 1822.

45 Ibid., May 17, 1824, December 2, 1844, January 20, 1845, June 9, 1845.

46 Ibid., August 5, 1850.

between three and five percent, with larger loans generally offered at lower interest rates.[47]

Thus, money was offered in virtually any amount, usually at competitive interest rates. Lenders generally required land or structures as collateral, and the mortgage market for freehold property became one of the most efficient capital markets in 18th century England.[48]

Because no comprehensive figures exist, the structure of firm sizes and of capital sources remains unknown, and consequently, we cannot safely assert that "average" entry costs were low. Indeed, evidence suggests that small workshops might not have been as small or as abundant as once assumed. Well before the capital-hungry railway boom, Birmingham enter-

---

[47] Ibid., May 17, 1824, April 16, 1838, December 2, 1844.

[48] Peter Mathias, The First Industrial Nation, Methuen and Co., London, 1969, 150. Funds were also lent privately. For example, John Smith Soden of Bath, a surgeon, lent Rice Harris, a Birmingham glass manufacturer, £5000 at five percent interest for an unspecified purpose. Item No. 461038, June 23, 1841, Birmingham Reference Library. Another surgeon, Richard Aston of Birmingham, lent £1000 to Joseph Fuller of nearby Digbeth at five percent interest, with title deeds as collateral for an unspecified purpose. Item No. 372045, February 10, 1826, Birmingham Reference Library. Private loans for either personal or business reasons were probably far more common than the number of surviving documents indicates.

prises attracted tens of thousands of pounds from local and distant investors.[49]

Although we know as little about uses of funds as sources, newspaper advertisements suggest no single receptacle for funds but rather a rich diversity of activities needing money. Breweries, dress shops, foundries, and a myriad of other establishments went to the market for funds. The only generalization that seems tenable is that neither workshops nor factories, hardware firms or retail outlets exerted disproportionate influence in finance. The Birmingham economy was far too complex for such concentrated forces.

Fixed and Working Capital

The varied capital markets seemed adequate for mobilizing fixed capital investments, but it is uncertain to what degree the banks,

---

49 Birmingham seems to have entered stock brokerage rather late. Not until 1845-6 are stockbroking firms (19) listed in Birmingham directories, by which time Liverpool had 85, Manchester 90, and Hull 52. As early as 1830, provincial towns like Bristol had one, Manchester two, and Liverpool four. The firms dealt mainly in shares of railway, bank, utility, and canal enterprises. J. R. Killick, W. Thomas, "The Provincial Stock Exchanges 1830-1870," Economic History Review, April 1970, 96.

partnerships, public and private loans, and savings clubs met the critical need for working capital among manufacturing firms, especially for wage payments. Short-term arrangements characterized commercial lending before the development of industrial banking, yet most saving and lending institutions failed to respond to the demand for working capital among manufacturers. Thus, investors offered large sums of capital during the 1830s and 1840s while Birmingham entrepreneurs raged at Parliament, and particularly the Bank of England, for failing to supply enough currency for daily transactions.[50]

The shortages of working capital threatened all entrepreneurs, but especially manufacturers, regardless of size. The currency crisis was so severe that Birmingham bankers like Thomas Attwood petitioned Parliament for years to lessen the problem. Parliament rarely responded satisfactorily.[51]

---

[50] Wright, Chronicles, 117.

[51] Ibid., 95,96,117. A Birmingham banker and founder of the Birmingham Political Union, Thomas Attwood argued vociferously for currency reform during the post-Napoleonic War years, proposing that Parliament fix the amount of currency not by bullion but by the level of employment. Parliament should provide enough currency for full employment, he argued. Asa Briggs, "Thomas Attwood and the Economic Background of the Birmingham Political Union," Cambridge Historical Journal, 1948, 190-216.

Partnerships were a form of long-run investment (14 to 21 years, typically) and not meant to provide working capital. Even though often used to expand trade rather than plant, partnership funds passed from manufacturer or merchant to other manufacturers or merchants, not from masters to men. Also, many partnerships simply combined business operations for efficiencies of operation rather than for infusions of new capital.

Savings clubs seemed intended more for personal than business purposes, and their generally small size precluded their use as rapidly turned over capital. Although undoubtedly helpful for the workers who joined them, they provided a relatively inflexible and low-paying form of placing money, however temporarily. Most likely, savings were used to pay for long run personal assets, like homes, or to cushion periods of unemployment.

Public and private loans, on the other hand, provided appropriate ways to finance either fixed capital or stocks, as suggested by the frequent resort of the Kenrick holloware firm to loans, especially during times of commercial difficulty. The Kenricks borrowed from friends, relatives, and bankers and repaid either on demand or over a period of years.[52]

---

52 Church, _Kenricks_, 46.

For the most part, entrepreneurs seem to have borrowed for specific, unexpected needs, rather than for normal operation. Because lenders sought land or structures as collateral, an entrepreneur dealing mostly with stocks rather than fixed capital could borrow only a small percentage of his needs or total worth. Because lenders often advertised both small and large sums, entrepreneurs perhaps relied on such funds for initial investment or for capital expansion, but more likely used them to acquire or improve personal assets, like homes and particularly land.

Retained earnings and trade credit seem the most important ways of financing fixed and working capital, using other sources as supplements. The Kenricks relied heavily on retained earnings throughout most of the early 19th century, though lump sum acquisitions like dowries were critical initially.

Because retained earnings financed only existing firms, trade credit would appear the sole recourse for a new entrepreneur with only his skills as collateral. Some entrepreneurs certainly could rely on trade credit, their own finesse, and luck in remaining solvent during sharp fluctuations in business to move up, but whether a large proportion of entrants could expect to follow this path remains moot. Even if large capital sums were not initially needed in Birmingham, trade cycles made entrepreneurship as risky as employment. Peter Mathias has suggested that few working class savers could accumulate enough funds to open lines of credit.[53] Thus most entrepreneurs, even in Birmingham, probably came from middle class families, a much smaller percentage of the population.

Several related issues bear close study. If fixed capital structures of firms in Birmingham and Manchester resembled each other in many respects, it is not unlikely that variable capital needs were also similar.

Textile operations, like those in Manchester, did not necessarily involve large capital size, even by contemporary standards. For 1795 Stanley D.Chapman found 50 Stockport cotton spinning workshops with insured valuation ranging from £50 to £2400, all well under the £5000 maximum he used to define "small" firms.[54] Of all the cotton manufacturing firms in England (except the Midlands) in 1795, Chapman found only 21 with insurance policy valuations over £10,000 and only 42 with valuations greater than £5000. Most of these firms were located in Manchester or nearby Stockport.[55] The largest, Robert Peel Sons and Partners, had eight calico works and 23 mills, valued at nearly £200,000, in Blackburn,

---

[53] Mathias, The First Industrial Nation, 156-7.

[54] Chapman, "Fixed Capital Formation", 261, 246.

[55] Ibid., 256-7.

Bury, Bolton, Burton, and Tamworth, but none in Manchester. Even the famous Ashworth cotton firm, which consisted solely of the New Eagley Mill near Bolton, was valued only at £3000 in 1817. Boyson estimated the initial cost at about £2000 for the mill, machinery, and stock in 1802.[56] Of the 185 cotton and wollen mills in 1803 employing over 20 work-people and over three apprentices and thus required to register under Peel's factory act of the same year, 65, employing 8475 workers, were located in Manchester.[57] As late as 1818 six Manchester factories employed over 600 workers.[58]

Between 1786 and 1799 (1793 omitted) the fixed capital component of total costs at the Pleasley Mills of Oldknow, Cowpe and Company ranged from a high of 90 percent in 1786 to a low of 34 percent in 1797. In nine of those

---

56 Boyson, Rhodes, The Ashworth Cotton Enterprise: The Rise and Fall of a Family Firm, 1818-1880, Oxford at the Clarendon Press, 1970, 8.

57 R. S. Fitton, A. P. Wadsworth, The Strutts and the Arkwrights, 1758-1830: A Study of the Early Factory System, Manchester University Press, 1958, 192n.

58 Ibid., 195.

thirteen years, the percentage was 60 percent or less.[59]

As the following table suggests, even during the mid-18th century costs of beginning business in several trades equalled or surpassed those in textiles.

---

59 Stanley D. Chapman, The Early Factory Masters: The Transition to the Factory System in the Midlands Textile Industry, David & Charles, Newton Abbot, 1967, 125-6. Chapman argued that cotton had low fixed capital requirements because mills, workshops, labor skills and other factors were easily converted from other uses. Chapman "Fixed Capital Formation", 252. Textile merchant firms supplied most capital for fixed investment. Ibid., 253. Peter Mathias noted that fixed capital rarely accounted for more than one-seventh total assets in early factories like textiles and brewing and only about half in heavy industries like iron and coal. Mathias, First Industrial Nation, 148.

FIXED COSTS FOR VARIOUS TRADES

Names of Trades	£ Sums necessary to set up as Master		
Appraiser	50	to	2000
Attorney	100	to	1000
Baker	100	to	500
Bellows Maker	10	to	100
Brazier	100	to	1000
____ of Silver & Gold		to	50
Button Ring Maker	5	to	10
Carpenter of Houses	50	to	500
Cheesemongers	100	to	500
Coach Makers	500	to	3000
Coopers	200	to	500
Cutler	50	to	200
Enameler	50	to	100
Engine Maker	500	to	2000
Edge-Tool Makers	50	to	100
Founders of Grates	50	to	500
Goldsmith	500	to	3000
Grocer	500	to	2000
Gun Smith	100	to	1000
Haberdashers	100	to	2000
Jewellers	100	to	5000
Ironmongers	500	to	2000
Linen Draper	1000	to	5000
Milliners	100	to	1000
Mercer	1000	to	10,000
Pattern Drawer		to	100
Plumber	100	to	500
Pin Maker	50	to	200
Screw Maker	20	to	50
Scale Maker	100	to	500
____ for Files	50	to	100
Stationer	100	to	2000
Taylor		to	500
Tea Shop	300	to	1000
Tobacconist	100	to	5000
Wire Drawer	100	to	200
Woolen Draper	1000	to	5000

Source: R. Campbell, The London Tradesmen (1747), p. 331-340.

Thus, merchanting, services and luxury trades, like mercers, haberdashers, linen and woollen drapers, grocers, tobacconists, stationers, attorneys, appraisers, coach makers and goldsmiths often required substantial investments. Even hardware trades like braziers, engine makers, gunsmiths, ironmongers, and plumbers called for several hundred pounds to set up. Significantly, sums cited in this table apply only to entry and do not represent average capital sizes of established firms. Thus, investment needed in textiles could well have required little more capital than needed for other businesses.

If costs of entry into the cloth trade were lower than once thought, close inspection shows entry costs for hardwares and other Birmingham industries higher. Drawn from the few surviving records of Birmingham partnership documents, the following table indicates the total capital values of several types of firms when partnership contracts were signed.

Date	Names of Partners	Partnership's Economic Activity	£ Capital Value*	
1825 LC	W. Lort W. Bragg	making steel trusses, surgical instruments, artificial limbs, glaziers, vices, moulds	624 312	936
1822 LC	E. Biggs W. Lee	wire drawering, metal rollering, mfg. of metallic goods and wares	1000 2000	3000
1806 LC	J. Dunderdale J. Mabson _. Labron	gunmaking & factoring		15,000
1808 LC	R. Stokes H. Hunt	merchanting	3000 2000	5000
1814 LC	J. Armitage J. Clarke	chemists & refining	3000 3000	6000
1822 LC	J. Crompton G. Blyth	merchant, factor, commission agents	4000	4000+
1804 LC	D. Hughes T. Fearon	glass mfg.	1000 1000	2000
1818 LC	W. Hutton M. Houghton	plating	1760+	2000 extra available

Date	Names of Partners	Partnership's Economic Activity	£ Capital Value*	
1814 LC	J. Simmons J. Parkes J. Simmons Green	merchanting	700 700 700	2100
1822 LC	J. Phipson B. Doughty	button mfg.	4000 1000	5000
1839 WH	H. Savage W. Allcock (bought out S. Savage & added £1000 each)	edge tool mfg.	500 500	1000*
1849 WH	B. Evans J. Gibbs C. Canning	coal master: buck & pipe making	7000 2000 2000	11,000
1806 LC	T. Hornblower J. Rose (dissolution)		4135 owed T. Hornblower	
1820 LC	J. James J. Gibbs (dissolution)	plating	3171 352	3523
1825 LC	W. Broadfield T. P. Broadfield S. Broadfield	boat building	900	

*
Capital value includes money, stock, credit, buildings, effects.

LC= Lee Crowder Collection, Birmingham Reference Library

WH= West Hagley Collection, Birmingham Reference Library.

Thus, Birmingham had many firms with capital values greater than £5000. As revealed in the partnership documents, Dunderdale, Mabson, and Labron, Birmingham gunmakers and factors, set up their firm during the Napoleonic Wars with over £15,000 in money and stock in trade.[60] The merchant firm of Stokes and Hunt was set up during this period with a capitalization of £5000. By 1815 the Kenricks' assets, net of book debts, were worth £11,805.[61] By 1851 the capital value of the firm had risen to £50,285.[62]

In addition to the Boulton and Watt enterprise, Birmingham had other sizeable investments,

---

60
Chapman suggested that merchants provided critical funds in Midlands, Scottish, and Northern cotton mills, and Birmingham merchants probably provided the same for hardware workshops. Chapman, "Fixed Capital Formation", 249. The distinction between merchant and manufacturer in Birmingham was never clear. Commercial men of both stripes were naturally powerful in city affairs.

61
Church, Kenrick, 38.

62
Ibid., 40.

as the following table suggests.[63]

	Yr. founded	£ Capital
Birmingham Metal Co.	1781	20,000
Birmingham Mining & Manufacturing Co.	1790	50,000
Rose Copper Co.	1793	100,000

Thus, many large firms existed in Birmingham, even in employment terms. As early as 1755, Birmingham buttonmaker John Taylor employed about 500 persons, although the overwhelming majority of them worked on contract in their own premises.[64] G. C. Allen found that by 1860 factories employing 40 to 100 persons existed in the manufacture of items like brass, wrought-chain, buttons, pins, and edge tools and larger factories making pens, screws, tinplate, and rolling stock.[65]

Birmingham merchanting firms, which played an important role in financing small and large trade transactions, often needed sizeable trade

---

63 Sidney Pollard, The Genesis of Modern Management, Penguin, Middlesex, 1965, 104.

64 Eversley, "Industry and Trade," 95.

65 G. C. Allen, The Industrial Development of Birmingham and the Black Country, G. Allen and Unwin, London, 1929, 97.

capital and grew rapidly. William Chance and Edward Homer set up a partnership in 1771 as Birmingham hardware factors, dealing wholesale in such items as locks, chains, and spoons, with an initial capital of £1300. By 1801 "net balance in stock" was worth more than £22,000 and outside investments, net of loans, for 1798-1801 equalled almost £17,000.[66] Birmingham entrepreneurs also granted much credit. Samuel Thornley, a Birmingham dry salter, carried accounts ranging from a few pounds to several thousand pounds around 1800.[67] From 1783 to 1790 the merchant firm of Fox, Cotterill, and Francis (later Scholefield, Goodman) granted nearly £10,000 credit to a purchaser (agent) in Philadelphia.[68] From 1783 to 1787 the same partnership held an account ranging from a few hundred to three thousand pounds with an individual in Belfast.[69]

The presumed distinction between Manchester as a factory city and Birmingham as a workshop

---

66 Hugh Chance manuscript in Chance and Homer Collection, University of Birmingham.

67 Ledger of Samuel Thornley of Snow Hill, Birmingham, dry salter, 1795-1805, Warwickshire County Record Office.

68 Scholefield, Goodman Collection, item 51, University of Birmingham.

69 _Ibid_., item 6, Account book.

city was at least partly illusory, created a misleading stereotype, that in turn resulted in confusion and ambiguity about economic relations. Manchester did have some factories, which Birmingham lacked, but in financial rather than technical terms the differences become less important.

With some exceptions, industrialization in both cities proceeded along similar lines in many respects. On the basis of previous evidence, the case for mobility in Birmingham, which the purportedly low capital requirements suggested, remains unproven.

CHAPTER FOUR: BIRMINGHAM LABOR AND THE INDUSTRIALIZING EXPERIENCE

Definition of specific labor forces to be compared

If barriers to occupational mobility confronting Birmingham workers resembled impediments in other cities, affinities in other labor force characteristics, particularly skill levels, invite further inspection.

Bottlenecks in the supply of skilled workers, as evinced by relatively high wages, can greatly stimulate the development of labor-saving technology. Yet the traditional description of Birmingham stresses the importance of skilled labor along with little labor displacing technology. From this argument one might infer either that Birmingham had an abundance of skilled labor, with relatively low wages, or that labor-displacing technological change actually did occur. In fact, partial contemporary evidence suggests that skill requirements declined progressively and that technological unemployment threatened labor markets. Thus, to judge whether labor experienced a unique environment in Birmingham, one must consider, besides mobility, the three remaining points of difference discerned by Briggs which will be discussed in subsequent sections of this chapter: greater importance of skilled labor, non-skilled labor displacing technological change, and steadier employment due to occupational and industrial diversity.

Ideally this explicit comparison of Birmingham and Manchester should fit within the context of a substantial body of literature on the role of labor in economic growth, but scholars have only recently begun to appreciate the complexity of the subject. Like any factor of production, all labor is not the same and thus, for example, a serious shortage of engineers can exist amidst high general unemployment. Conversely, especially during periods of rapid growth, semi-skilled factory operatives can achieve relatively greater wage increases than skilled engineers if the market for the latter changes more slowly.

Taking a simplified approach and using the model developed by W. Arthur Lewis, Charles Kindleberger maintained that the rapidly growing Western economies in the post-war era succeeded largely because of the availability of large supplies of labor. He argued, with Lewis, that growth depended primarily on technology and industrial management, but that labor was a critical permissive factor.[1] With surplus labor wages will not increase fast enough to cut into profit, investment, and productivity.[2]

---

[1] Charles P. Kindleberger, Europe's Postwar Growth: The Role of Labor Supply, Harvard University Press, Cambridge, 1967, intro.

[2] Ibid., 3.

Reviewing the work of several authors, Kassalow severely criticized the Lewis model for focussing excessively on capital, despite research stressing human resource variables like education.[3] He also argued the case for shortages rather than surpluses of labor (via slow population growth), as in Japan and the Western economies compared with present under-developed areas.[4]

The simple two-sector model also ignores intermediate sectors and oversimplifies the labor supply. Thus, the Lewis model failed to include the kind of domestic and workshop enterprises that characterized much of the 19th century Western growth. Myint considered skilled labor so important that he suggested a model incorporating capital, labor, and skilled labor (including management).[5]

---

[3] Everett M. Kassalow, "Labor in Development: A Critique of Some Current Concepts," Proceedings of the 22nd Annual Meeting of the Industrial Relations Research Association, 1969, 271.

[4] Ibid., 271-2. Habakkuk, of course has argued that the relative scarcity of labor in the US induced more technological innovation than in Britain in the 19th century. H. J. Habakkuk, American and British Technology in the Nineteenth Century: the Search for Labour-Saving Inventions, Cambridge University Press, 1967, 196.

[5] Kassalow, 274.

If the contribution of labor to growth remains unclear, the impact of growth on labor remains no less ambiguous. As Landes has emphasized, industrialization abolishes some jobs and creates others.[6] Only close empirical investigation can unearth net gains or losses in the job market, suggesting that overaggregation only obfuscates the perplexing relationships between industrialization and labor markets. Units as amorphous as "Birmingham" and "Manchester" can only hinder analysis, for the two labor markets probably resembled each other in many sectors, such as retail trade. Thus, the investigator must sharply limit the bases of comparison to unique industries, sluicing the stubble to bare the lodes.

To provide perspective a brief view of employment structure on the national scene is warranted first, however. Industrial development in England stimulated extraordinary changes in the structure and composition of national output, yet on the whole it did not greatly alter the structure of employment. Workers in older industries, such as builders, shipbuilders, printers, cabinet makers, tailors, glass-bottle makers, bookbinders, coachmakers,

---

[6] D. Landes, The Unbound Prometheus, Cambridge University Press, 1970, 118.

and some engineers were little affected.[7]

Nationally, manufacturing grew most rapidly just after the Napoleonic Wars, employment in that activity rising from one-quarter of the gainfully occupied British population in 1811 to one-third by 1841, and remaining at roughly that proportion for the rest of the century.[8]

Between 1801 and 1831 agriculture gave way to manufacturing in relative importance, though the change slowed from 1825 to 1850. Mining, transportation, and trade, however, started to climb relatively and absolutely at this point. Employment in trade and commerce doubled from 1861 to 1891, and from 1841 to 1891 the numbers in trade as a percentage of the total gainfully occupied British population increased from 10 percent to a little over 15 percent.[9]

During the third quarter of the 19th century, merchanting and finance, transport, domestic service, and the professions grew,

---

[7] E. J. Hobsbawm, "The Labour Aristocracy in Nineteenth-Century Britain," Labouring Men, Anchor Books, 1967, 330.

[8] Phyllis Dean and W. A. Cole, British Economic Growth 1688-1959, Cambridge University Press, London, 1967, 144.

[9] Ibid.

while agriculture and manufacturing declined relatively.[10]

Although manufacturing as a whole grew relatively little from 1841 to 1861, specific industries gained. The percentage employed in machinery and tools more than doubled, while that in fuel, gas, and chemicals tripled. Within manufacturing, textiles and dyeing remained the largest single component, at about 10 percent of the entire labor force, with dress slightly behind. The percentage of workers in building remained a fairly constant five to six percent, while transport more than doubled to 4.6 percent.[11]

Yet by 1861 both national and major urban employment structures failed to reflect the vast changes that had occurred in output,as suggested in the following table:

---

[10] S. G. Checkland, The Rise of Industrial Society in England 1815-1885, Longmans, London, 1964, 218. See also, Charles Booth, "Occupations of the People of the United Kingdom, 1801-81," Journal of the Statistical Society, June 1886, 314-417.

[11] Booth, 414-5.

PRINCIPAL OCCUPATIONS IN ENGLAND AND WALES:

1861

Occupations	Persons
Agricultural Labourer, Farm Servant,and Sheperd	1,188,789
Domestic Servant	1,106,974
Cotton, Calico-manufacture, Printing and Dyeing	456,646
Labourer (Branch undefined)	309,883
Dressmaker and Milliner	287,101
Boot and Shoe Makers	250,581
Farmer, Grazier	249,745
Coal-Miner	246,613
Carpenter, Joiner	177,969
Laundry-keeper, Mangler Washerwoman	167,607
Seaman (Merchant Service)	159,469
Tailor	136,390
Woolen Cloth manufacture	130,034
Iron manufacture, Moulder Founder	125,771
Blacksmith	108,165
Satin, silk, manufacture	101,678
Grocer, Tea Dealer	93,483
Mason, Pavior	84,434
Bricklayer	79,458
Worsted manufacture	79,242

Source: Census 1861

Most surprising is not the lack of new trades but the strength of the old. Aside from domestic service and textiles which clearly led all other nonagricultural occupations, traditional jobs like boot and shoe makers, carpenters and joiners remained highly significant. The industrial revolution raised per capita incomes not only in relatively new industries, but also in auxiliary trades, like industrial services and construction,and in distribution. As new income diffused, grocers and tea dealers, for example, found new outlets in the prospering middle class, and clothing makers produced finer wares for a growing domestic market. Indeed, income growth even stimulated labor intensive services. Domestics fell from 16 percent of the work force in 1841 to 13 percent in 1851, but rose to nearly 16 percent in 1881.[12]

In Birmingham, traditional trades showed little sign of dying. Following the national pattern closely, construction, personal service, and distributive trades grew, along with newer nonindustrial occupations like commercial clerking and warehousing: and industrial occupations that had led in the first part of the century, guns, brass, jewellery, and buttons, remained important.

---

12 Booth, 414-5.

PRINCIPAL OCCUPATIONS IN BIRMINGHAM
1861

Occupations	Persons
Domestic Servants	8779
Brassfounder, manufacture	6215
Shoemaker, Bootmaker	5315
Gunsmith	5107
Buttonmaker	5079
Others in brass and other mixed metals	4946
Milliner, Dressmakers	4588
Goldsmith, Jeweller	4386
Labourer	4334
Laundress	2375
Tailor	2225
Warehouseman and woman (but not Manchester warehouseman)	2191
Iron manufacture	2163
Carpenter, Joiner	2092
Messenger, Porter, Errand Boy and Girl	2062
Engine and Machine Maker	1964
Others in Iron manufacture	1960
Bricklayer	1849
Blacksmith	1781
Commercial Clerk	1564

Source: compiled from Census of England and Wales 1861.

Even Manchester, the archetypal industrial city, showed striking lack of novelty in its major occupations in mid-century.

PRINCIPAL OCCUPATIONS IN MANCHESTER (CITY)
AND SALFORD (BOROUGH)
MALES 20 YEARS OF AGE AND OVER
1861

Occupations	Persons
Cotton manufacture	10,133
Labourer	5781
Iron manufacture	4637
Shoemaker, Bootmaker	3787
Carpenter, Joiner	3695
Engine and Machine Maker	3338
Tailor	3004
Commercial Clerk	2574
Carman, Carter, Carrier, Drayman	2529
Plumber, Painter, Glazier	2472
Messenger, Porter, Errand Boy	2434
Warehouseman (not Manchester warehouseman)	2250
Blacksmiths	1854
Silk manufacture	1702
Bricklayer	1490
Calico, Cotton-Printer	1325
Calico, Cotton-Dyer	1284
Railway Servant	1265
Mechanic	1242
Cabinet Maker, Upholsterer	1223

Source: Census of England and Wales 1861.

Focussing on adult males, the table closely parallels the nation and Birmingham. Transportation and textiles protrude a bit more, but storage, distribution, and construction bulk large. Thus, Birmingham and Manchester differed by their respective emphases on hardwares and textiles but were similar in many other categories.

It is necessary to introduce a methodological note here, for two major problems arise in defining specific labor forces to be compared: determining the appropriate aggregate labor force and determining the appropriate industries. Nineteenth century census officials seemed more concerned with classifying the population than with determining labor force participation rates. Thus the term "occupied" included everyone, and indeed seemed to mean "classified" rather than "gainfully employed." For example, wives and widows not otherwise described in one of the 434 activities listed in the Census were nonetheless considered part of the occupied population. Even "scholars" (generally boys at school) were occupied. Yet defining such comprehensive compartments is misleading, for such a classification ignores the diversity of work in preindustrial and industrial society. Then as now, seasonal or trade fluctuations made many jobs part-time, especially when performed at home. Industrializing economies thus required large labor reserves, mostly women and children, as social overhead.

Supplies of women and children nourished the capacity of the system to respond to spurts in trade and investment in both textile and hardware industries, which employed large numbers of women and children under less than full employment conditions. Because housework was postponable and schoolwork optional, women and children could work in many different trades irregularly throughout the year, without fundamentally altering their primary indentification with home or school. Even pre-school age children could perform many simple tasks that required neither skill nor prolonged attention.

Thus it seems more appropriate to consider the entire population as the relevant (potential and actual) labor force than to compute a net figure by subtracting "occupied" groups like wives and widows not otherwise counted and scholars. There seems no obvious bias in using such a technique for both Birmingham and Manchester and something to be gained from this more inclusive approach.

To net these labor subgroups from some arbitrarily defined concept of the labor force would disguise the most important aspect of labor in the nineteenth century - its flexibility. Indeed, the very difficulty of defining a distinct labor force reflects the ambiguities of pre-industrial societies transforming themselves into industrial societies. The labor force was never clearly defined because work was never clearly defined. Who performed tasks was not as important as having the tasks done.

Precisely defining industries to be compared also presented conceptual and operational problems. What exactly is a hardware industry? Does it include crude nailmakers as well as fine jewellers, surgical instrument makers as well as gunstock hewers? Should the industry be defined by its end products (nails, watches), by the functions of its end products (building machines, killing Napoleon's soldiers), or by production processes (stamping trinkets, extruding gun barrels)? Is a gun a hardware item because it is composed of nails and formed with edge tools? Or does its military function change its classification?

The ambiguity surrounding such examples stresses the difficulty of narrowly defining any economic activity. The tightness of interstices among industries mocks attempts to pick apart the webbing, forcing us to consider natural complexes of industries rather than artificial, partial industry groups. From this locus the only reasonable approach seems to be to focus on the nature of materials (with necessary qualifications) rather than end products, production processes, or functions. Thus, one might define the hardware industry as one dealing primarily with producing metal goods, for whatever purposes, excluding primary production, except brass because statistics do not allow easy separation. Textile industries would include establishments making, processing, and cutting cloth, excluding those making clothes.

Based on such definitions, the following tables, derived from the Census of 1861, localize differences between Manchester (and Salford) and Birmingham as sharply as possible.

Census Code	Salford & Manchester Textiles	
XI (1)	Wool and Worsted	1,038
(2)	Silk	7,859
(3)	Cotton and Flax	51,322
(4)	Mixed materials	8,175
		68,394

Above Textile workers as a percent of total population $\frac{68,394}{460,428} \approx 15\%$

Census Code	Birmingham Hardwares	
X (6)	Designs, Medals and Dies	226
(7)	Watches and Scientific instruments	1,521
(8)	Surgical instruments	37
(9)	Arms	5,834
(10)	Machines and Tools	6,168
(16)	Implements	439
XI (5)	Dress -buttonmaking	5,079
XV (8)	Gold, Silver and precious stones	7,011
(13)	Brass and other mixed Metals	13,804
(14)	Iron manufactures	4,259
		44,378

Hardware workers as percent of the total population $\frac{44,378}{196,076} \approx 23\%$

Thus, textiles in the Manchester area employed about 15 percent of the population and hardwares in Birmingham employed about 23 percent. Although hardwares might seem more important to Birmingham than textiles to Manchester, if the 30,308 workers in dress and the 996 workers in hemp and other fibrous materials were added, differences would narrow significantly. Most important are the following points:

One, in neither case did "unique" industries employ more than a quarter of the total population. If some workers found themselves in textiles or hardwares, the average worker did not.

Two, despite the neatness of the classification, all qualifications regarding definitions still hold in addition to other investigational problems. Both textiles and hardwares were extremely complex in industrial structure, organization, financing, and labor force, warning us to make judgements cautiously. Problems with aggregation remain, though perhaps in reduced form.

Three, the tables say nothing of related industries. Thus, an engineering industry of some note developed in Manchester to build and service textile machinery, for example.

However, despite these conceptual and theoretical problems, we now have a reasonably well based foundation for beginning to compare the impact of industrialization on workers in Birmingham hardwares and Manchester textiles. We must now return to the crux of the argument: why skilled workers attracted attention in the first place.

Concerned mostly with the social effects of industrialization, the traditional argument claimed that a large proportion of the Birmingham workforce was skilled, with relatively high earnings, thus explaining the general lack of social tensions in the city. Although social tensions do indeed seem to have occurred less often or less obviously in Birmingham than in Manchester, other factors like weak trade unions and common political ideologies could explain such relative calm.

Thus the size and income of the skilled working group might explain little of the city's social peace. Nonetheless, the argument stands until refuted, impelling the critic to take two basic steps: one, measure the relative importance of skilled labor: two, identify and, if necessary, explain differences in wages. If the traditional explanation is correct, both the relative number and wage levels of Birmingham skilled workers should far exceed those of skilled workers in Manchester.

Even if expectations about mobility were based partly on myth, such a large proportion of non-ostentatiously comfortable citizens could have acted as a formidable social damper in times of stress. The hypothesis thus propounded, we must begin the analysis of historical circumstances to test it.

Skilled Workers: Quality and Quantity

Definition and Identification of Skilled Workers

The relationships between economic growth and occupational change are not clear, for labor demand depends on the nature of production processes in new and allied older industries and the direction of this demand is not uniform. New labor forces do not necessarily differ in size or remuneration from the old, and established occupations do not always disappear.

For example, the development of railroads increased the demand for engineers, some of whom were drawn from public works projects, and for building tradesmen to construct the roads and also new buildings in areas stimulated by the new transportation outlet. Thus, changes in the structure, composition, and size of output do not necessarily induce similar changes in employment, and because the industrial revolution brought few shifts in occupational structures one would expect few shifts in skill structures. Indeed, before and during the industrial revolution, hardware and textile production required similar skills in many areas. For example, engineers made both textile machinery and steam engines, and mechanics, who built and repaired rudimentary self-acting mechanisms, found work in either the North or the Midlands.

Several methods of defining skilled labor unique and common to both industries are possible.

One, we might look at wage differentials, which would point to the most productive or powerful labor groups. For the traditionally skilled building trades workers, the task seems easy. For the newer hardware and textile trades, however, the difficulties are imposing, partly because of the prevalence of piece rates and partly because job content changed rapidly even if job titles did not. Nonetheless, such a wage structure has its uses.

Two, we could study trade union membership, which would strongly point to skilled workers in an era innocent of industrial unionism. Craft workers found organization incomparably easier than semi-skilled and unskilled operatives until such lesser talented groups amassed greater power in the late 19th century. However Birmingham had few unions, a topic of much interest for later discussion, but one which limits the value of the present analysis.

Three, we could devise a crude but easily measurable index to give at least a first approximation of the dimensions of the skilled labor force. An index based on the percentage of men in a given industrial or occupational group might well provide such a measure because virtually no women and children achieved high skill levels and at least some men did. One could also perhaps adapt ratios found in the Select Committee on Manufactures report of 1833, cited by Sidney Pollard, which observed that for each man doing the highest quality work there were three doing medium and eight doing common work in Sheffield metal trades. It seems more reliable, however, to inspect historical evidence rather than rely on such general assessments.[13] Thus an industry or occupation with relatively more men than women and children probably had a higher skill level on average. Because this method has fewer definitional and operational flaws than the other two, it seems most appropriate here. Before beginning this specific analysis, however, it will be useful for perspective to survey other attempts to define skilled labor.

Generalizing broadly for the early

---

13 Sidney Pollard, A History of Labour in Sheffield, Liverpool University Press, 1959, 60n.

Victorian national economy, J. F. C. Harrison ranked trade skills using the structure of wages approach. Thus, artisans steadily earning between 30 and 40s a week were "very highly skilled". Within this group, distinctions existed between "society" and "nonsociety" men, that is, the very skilled and the lesser skilled in the same trade. For example, he estimated that 600 to 700 London cabinet makers made high quality cabinets, while 4000 to 5000 produced for the mass market. About ten percent in a given trade, society men belonged to trade unions and usually served apprenticeships, but nonsociety men were usually much less skilled and organized. Thus, in more traditional trades skilled men were printing compositors, breeches-makers, jewellers, watch-makers, scientific instrument makers, some cutlery workers, hatters, iron molders, shipwrights and carpenters. In new trades, society men were locomotive engineers, first class fine cotton spinners, and calico printers and dyers. This labor aristocracy resembled small shopkeepers or independent masters in status and presumably in income.[14]

Harrison next defined a group of "ordinary skilled workers", earning from 20s to 30s a week and including occupations like some types of building tradesmen, craftsmen, tailors, shoe-

---

[14] Harrison, The Early Victorians, 24.

makers, skilled engineers, and lower grade spinners. Although artisans,these men had less regular employment and lower wages than very highly skilled workmen.[15]

A very heterogeneous group, semi-skilled and unskilled workers differed completely from the other two classifications. Prevented by trade unions from doing skilled work, these laborers generally earned one-third to one-half skilled earnings.[16]

The interrelations of this nonskilled group wove a complex tapestry. Although less skilled than handloom weavers, for example, railway navvies generally earned more because of the arduous work and the demand for their labor.[17] Regional and occupational variations also occurred. For example, only the North had large numbers of factory hands and only London had many street traders.

Job environments and wages varied within industries. In textiles, work and wages differed according to branch of industry (cotton, wool,worsted, flax, silk), pace of technological change, employment of women and children, and unemployment. Thus, the income of a male factory worker in Yorkshire or Lancashire could vary from 14s

---

15 <u>Ibid</u>., 25.

16 <u>Ibid</u>.

17 <u>Ibid</u>., 26.

to 22s a week; women earned 5s to 10s a week and children about half as much.[18]

Many factory jobs paid far better wages than traditional skilled occupations. Leeds wool sorters earned about 21s a week, compared with about 16s a week for tailors and about 14s a week for shoemakers.[19]

Sensitive to many natural and economic factors,employment for most nonskilled workers fluctuated greatly. Especially during the 1830s and 1840s, laborers relied heavily on poor relief. In 1844 over nine percent of the total population received indoor or outdoor relief.[20] Weather conditions set the pace of employment for building trades workers, agricultural workers, and street sellers, and fashion changes caused much unemployment for tailors, boot and shoemakers, milliners and others.[21]

The middle class represented only a small proportion of the population. At about £60 a year, clerks or teachers generally earned less than skilled artisans, but a lower middle class household usually took in about £150 to £200 a year, far above even the most able artisans.[22]

---

[18] *Ibid*., 28.

[19] *Ibid*.

[20] *Ibid*., 48.

[21] *Ibid*., 49

[22] *Ibid*., 104.

Also trying to rank incomes for the mid 19th century, Leone Levi listed those trades in which some workers earned forty or more shillings a week, to single out the most skilled.

TRADES IN 1865 WITH WEEKLY WAGE-RTAES

OF 40 SHILLINGS AND ABOVE

Dockyards	Leather
Railways	Glass
Bookbinding	Printing
Scientific Instruments	Musical Instrument Makers
Cutlery	Lithographers
Shipbuilding	Woodcarvers
Cabinet-makers	Watchmakers
Hatters	Hosiery
Jewellery	Bone and Ivory Turners
Iron	Pottery
Textiles	Steel

Source: From Leone Levi, Wages and Earnings of the Working Classes (1867), as reprinted in E. J. Hobsbawm, "The Labour Aristocracy in Nineteenth-Century Britain", Labouring Men, Anchor Books, New York, 1964, 331.

Several patterns emerge. Industries leading the industrial revolution, iron and textiles, remained important as wage leaders well after the industrial revolution matured. Transportation and transportation-related industries, like dockyards, railways, and shipbuilding, were also prominent. Yet growth in these newer sectors did not appreciably alter the wage status of older trades. Production of highly skill-intensive, quality consumer goods continued to employ and pay well, cabinet makers, hatters, musical instrument makers, lithographers, woodcarvers, watchmakers, bone and ivory turners, makers of pottery, cutlery, scientific instruments, hosiery, leather, and glass. Because of a growing market for printed materials, printers and bookbinders also prospered. Although only some workers earned forty shillings or more a week (using Harrison's interpretation this would mean about 10 percent in each industry), the list offers a guide to the employment of skilled labor in the economy by suggesting which industries attracted the most talented members of the labor force.

Levi's data suggest that highly skilled labor characterized many new and old industries, implying that industrial change did not result in a general downgrading of skills, at least for some workers. Although textiles ranks explicitly as a high wage employer for some employees, none of the diverse Birmingham hardware trades achieve mention. Perhaps gathering data proved too difficult for Levi. Perhaps also, the data simply did not reflect high wages.

Neither Harrison nor Levi developed definitions but relied almost entirely on wage levels instead of job content to define skilled work. Without detailed data about the nature of work, however, even occupational titles can mislead. Producing a bewildering variety of goods, Birmingham tradesmen fell under a vast constellation of job titles, which often masked job content. Thus, for example, blacksmiths in Wolverhampton and neighborhood in 1840 earned 25s.a week in the edge tool trade, but 30s. a week making iron hurdles and bedsteads.[23] Similarly, forgers in stocks and locks earned 20s. a week but those in file and edge tool making earned fifty percent more.[24]

Each trade also had its unique jobs. Thus, in 1840 the Wolverhampton stock lock industry needed key turners, the edge tool industry hoe makers, and the iron foundry and holloware industry holloware enamellers.[25]

Within Birmingham, mechanical trades prospered relatively. In a return of 791 members of a provident institution (the vast

---

[23] Board of Trade, Returns of Wages published between 1830 and 1886, 1887, 197, 196.

[24] Ibid., 197.

[25] Ibid.

majority of them children whose parents had set up savings accounts for them), the most common occupation, brass and copper working, claimed one-third, and the second most common, iron, took over 10 percent.[26]

Another return from the same provident institution, covering only mechanical trades, disclosed average weekly wages for 199 men in 1840 of 24s. 3d., well within the "lesser skilled" category suggested by Harrison. The range of wages was great: Among men 21 to 25 years of age, wages varied from 14s. to 40s. per week, averaging 24s. 2d.[27]

Ames and Rosenberg have suggested that the skill content of jobs be determined by the number of distinct judgements a worker must make. Thus, a worker who performs different operations makes many different judgements and can thus be considered skilled.[28]

---

26 "Contributions to the Economical Statistics of Birmingham," Journal of the Statistical Society, January 1840, 437.

27 If the average of 24s 3d. in this survey were not weighted, the true figure might fall even lower. The author also fixed 40s. as an upper bound for most mechanics, and justified the credibility of the return because the low wages reported seemed realistic. "Contributions to the Economical Statistics of Birmingham", 437.

28 E. Ames, N. Rosenberg, "The Progressive Division and Specialization of Industries", Journal of Development Studies, July 1965, 263-83.

Because of the enormous diversity of tasks in Birmingham, few job descriptions exist, although parliamentary inquiries like the Children's Employment Commission suggested that many hardware jobs required little talent.

Precluded from comparing skills solely on the basis of wage statistics or job content, we must use cruder distinctions. By default then, the most useful approach involves comparing textiles and hardwares according to the percentage of men in specific trades. As mentioned, without doubt women and children had few if any skills, and skilled workers were almost always men.

The impact of industrialization on a labor force depends heavily on the demographic structure of the labor market. Households felt economic fluctuation more severely if the chief earner, usually the adult male, lost his wages. Thus, in volatile industries like textiles a predominence of men would have heightened tension during downswings, particularly if they held low paying positions. Yet the textile industry had a highly diversified workforce, with men prominent only in some sectors:

MANCHESTER AND SALFORD: TEXTILES, 1861

Census Code	Industry	Total M & F	Total $M \geq 20$	$M \geq 20$ as £ total labor force in this industry
X1 (1)	Wool and worsted	1,038	522	50.2
(2)	Silk	7,859	2,231	28.3
(3)	Cotton and Flax	51,322	14,806	28.8
(4)	Mixed materials (1,2,3)	8,175	3,645	44.5
(5)	Dress	30,308	8,609	28.4
(6)	Hemp and other fibrous materials	996	479	48.0
Total and average		99,698	30,292	30.3

M - Males

F - Females

Source: figures computed from Census of England and Wales 1861

Cotton and flax, the single greatest employer in textiles with just over half of the textile labor force, vied with dress as a relatively minor employer of men, although the two sectors differed fundamentally in technology and organization. In cotton and flax, of course, new machinery and swarms of workers contrasted with the more traditional work environment of domestic sweatshops in apparel. The largest employee groups within clothing were milliners and dressmakers (exclusively women) and shoemakers and bootmakers (men and women), with tailors following close behind (nearly all men). The apparel trades catered to a well-heeled middle class clientele and produced largely for custom until the late 19th century. In any case, women and children played a far greater role in textiles overall than men, accounting for nearly 70 percent of the labor force, and within specific enterprises the proportion rose even higher.[29] Men provided the skills, working as machine printers and foremen, for example.

Thus, trade fluctuations would probably affect secondary workers (women and children) far more severely than primary workers (men), for employers in the highly competitive textile industry could not afford to treat scarce, skilled labor capriciously.

In the most important Birmingham hardware industries men seemed to play a greater role, although the skill implications are not clear:

---

[29] D. Chadwick, "On the Rate of Wages in Manchester and Salford, and the Manufacturing Districts of Lancashire, 1839-59," Journal of the Statistical Society, March, 1860, 5.

BIRMINGHAM HARDWARE INDUSTRY

Census Code	Industry	Total M & F	Total M ≥ 20	M≥20 as % total labor force in this industry
X (9)	Arms	5,834	3,747	64.2
(10)	Machines & Tools	6,168	3,727	60.4
XI (5)	Dress - buttonmaking	5,079	1,526	30.0
XV (8)	Gold, Silver & precious stones	7,011	3,419	48.7
(13)	Brass and other mixed metals	13,804	7,507	54.3
(14)	Iron manufactures	8,856	4,259	48.0
Total and average		46,752	24,185	51.7

M - Males

F - Females

Source: figures computed from Census of 1861

Birmingham hardwares employed relatively more men than Manchester textiles, one half compared with one third. At first glance, this phenomenon suggests that hardwares required more highly skilled labor than textiles. Inspection of occupations in allied and more general sectors raises questions, however.

Although Manchester had relatively fewer general laborers and relatively more young males in school, the differences with Birmingham were insignificant. In both cases laborers accounted for about five percent of all men and "scholars" for about a third of all boys. More compelling patterns emerge from the Manchester characteristic of employing relatively more men in skilled mechanical trades which were considered uniquely important to Birmingham. Although Birmingham had a higher percentage of its total adult male labor force in the machine and tool industry (4.9 percent versus 3.8 percent), within that particular industry labor force Manchester employed relatively more men. Thus, men were 74.6 percent of the machine-and tool-making employees in Manchester but 60.4 percent in Birmingham, a relative difference of about one-quarter. As a percentage of its total adult male workforce, moreover, Manchester employed 20 percent more men in implements and two-thirds more in mercantile pursuits.[30] As a less direct indication of relative skill levels, one can look at trade union membership in skilled trades. In 1859 the Amalgamated Society of Engineers had seven branches in Manchester with a total of 1442 members. Birmingham had one branch with only 216 members.[31] With about 25 percent more workers, Manchester had almost 600 percent more engineers, the most highly skilled mechanical workers, in trade unions. Even the general lack of enthusiasm of Birmingham workers for unions could not explain such a difference. Birmingham seems to have had fewer engineers and perhaps fewer skilled workers in general.

30

Percentages of All Adult Males

Census Code	Activity	Manchester & Salford	Birmingham
VI (1)	Mercantile men	5.0	2.9
X (16)	Implements	.6	.5

Source: Census of 1861.

31
Amalgamated Society of Engineers Monthly Report, July 1859, item HM 1331, University of Birmingham.

The very impasses confronted along this jagged trek suggest one major theme: one cannot categorically state that Birmingham had more skilled men relatively or absolutely than Manchester. We simply know too little of actual historical circumstances at the moment to generalize. This ambiguity, however, raises questions of its own about the nature of the labor supply in Birmingham. Why, for example, did reputedly more labor intensive workshops fail to demand clearly a more highly skilled workforce?

If technological and organization forms changed little in Birmingham during the industrial revolution, one would expect traditional skills to have passed down through generations of artisans, with skilled workers relatively as important in the mid-19th century as in mid-18th. The thrust of economic change seems confused. As just noted, women and children played important roles in several hardware sectors by 1861, suggesting either that technology and the low skill levels remained unchanged or that technology changed and skills decreased in absolute and relative importance. To understand the complex forces acting on the Birmingham labor force an investigation of technology seems imperative.

<u>Technological Change</u>

Contemporary evidence suggests that technological change greatly affected the traditional skilled areas in metal working at national and local levels, and must not be underestimated in Birmingham. Although the most striking technological and organizational changes occurred in textiles, coal, and iron, other sectors, such as engineering, also changed greatly during the early 19th century.

Workers in traditional occupations, like millwrights, blacksmiths, carpenters, and masons built much of the machinery of the industrial revolution, but such handwork created bottlenecks as the demand for engineering goods rose, and much effort in the early part of the century sought to make production tasks simpler.[32]

For example, the lathe and the planer, the most basic engineering tools, received much attention. In 1800 Henry Maudsley solved the problem of making plane surfaces easily by developing an all-metal slide rest to replace wooden lathes run by hand or foot, and other improvements soon followed.[33] Between 1815 and 1840 several innovations made the planer

---

32 J. B. Jefferys, <u>The Story of Engineers, 1800-1945</u>, Lawrence and Wishart, reprinted by the Johnson Reprint Corporation, New York and London, 1970, 10, 12.

33 <u>Ibid</u>., 13.

much more accurate, and reduced the need for human judgment.[34]

Related developments also occurred. By 1840 shapers, slotters, borers, and self-acting drills were made of metal rather than wood, and engines were used to run the machines. Developments in the cast iron industry to allow cheap production of parts of machines, shafts, pulleys, and gears of metal rather than of wood proved indispensible to progress in tool and machine making.[35]

Such innovations naturally affected the demand for labor, as engineering began to subdivide into more specialized tasks, and occupations like pattern-makers, hammermen, firemen, turners, and planers replaced millwrights, carpenters, and blacksmiths.[36]

New and much less skilled engineers, who actually served as machine tenders, replaced skilled millwrights in many jobs. For example, in the Salford area in 1841, self-acting machines and tools required no direct supervision at all, allowing laborers earning 12 to 14s. a week to operate planing machines.

---

[34] Ibid., 13-14.

[35] Ibid., 14.

[36] Ibid., 15.

In London in the 1820s, semiskilled labor earning about 18s. a week replaced millwrights earning about 40s.[37] Although skilled labor still performed many operations, unskilled and semiskilled workers performed a growing proportion of the tasks in machine making.

By mid-19th century some contemporaries had noted that the piece-work system had driven wages and prices to far lower levels than before.[38] The nature of production forced workmen in the highly competitive hardware industry to trade off high income (actually profit, for most were piece-workers) per unit for volume.[39] The pressure to cut costs encouraged specialization of tasks and thus the use of unskilled labor in the production if not designing process. Women and especially children provided ideal sources.

Such employment opportunities for the unskilled had deep ramifications. Thomas Becket of Messrs. Beckett Brothers', Tin-Plate Workers, felt that many families moved to Birmingham because young persons could easily find jobs, often earning half as much as men (a commentary on the low incomes of males) and, consequently, the city also had a large supply of unskilled heads of households.[40]

---

37 Ibid., 16.

38 Children's Employment Commission, Third Report of the Commission, 1864, 66.

39 R. F. Martineau to H. Martineau, August 14, 1859.

40 Children's Employment Commission, Third Report, 84-5.

Because of this unskilled adult labor pool, some manufacturers did not feel threatened by child labor legislation, which would probably not reduce drastically the number of unskilled workers available on short-term call. According to J.E. White, who prepared the report of the Children's Employment Commission, the "great resemblance of many of the processes of work in different trades, or the small amount of skill and training required, or both of these causes," greatly eased the acquiring of extra hands when needed.[41]

This supply of unskilled labor also affected the choice of technology used by Birmingham entrepreneurs, for children were often employed as machine-tenders.

Technological change in Birmingham did not take the highly visible form of massive factories, but acted no less dramatically in altering the nature of hand trades. Innovations were small, closely tied to daily work experience, but significant enough to seem to have lessened the need for skilled labor.

By mid-century some types of hardware machinery enabled production to flow with little need for highly-trained supervision. In making some of the most common items, such as hooks and eyes, screws,

---

[41] *Ibid.*, 51.

and buttons, technology played a critical role. Also, according to White:

> Many of the machines. . . are made, are fed, attended, and cleaned by boys, girls, women, one person sometimes attending a considerable number. . . .[42]

The technology lent itself easily to low skill, specialization operation. Although most workers used steam machinery to some degree, much simpler aids, like stamps, presses, files, and hammers were also common. Steam power was often harnessed to these tools, as with pulleys or stamps, to allow operation by women and children.[43]

Although Birmingham adopted few of the major innovations that characterized the industrial revolution in iron, coal, and textiles, it made significant advance in small-scale technology. R. B. Prosser calculated that Birmingham had generated more than its share of patents in the 19th century, and R. F. Martineau, a Birmingham industrialist, noted that such simple devices as improved stamping machines had drastically downgraded skilled labor, which, of course, also reduced strike

---

42 Ibid., 55.

43 Ibid.

risks.[44] Thus, not only did the production process demand fewer skills by mid-century, but women and children played an important, even critical role, as the following sample for 1841 indicates.[45]

Activity	Women and Children (%)
Japanners and lacquerers	57
Steel pen makers	88
Screwmakers	79
Buttonmakers	62
Steelworkers	46
Brassfounders and moulders	26
File cutters and makers	26
Founders (branch not specified)	35

By 1861 the situation had changed little. In five of the first ten Birmingham occupations in 1861, the proportion of women and children stood remarkably high. Males under 20 comprised over one-third the work force among brass founders and manufacturers and gunsmiths and gun manufacturers. Men were just over one-third the buttonmakers, well under half those listed as

---

44 R. B. Prosser, Birmingham Inventors and Inventions, "Journal" Printing Works, Birmingham, 1881. Birmingham Reference Library, Only 50 copies were printed. R. F. Martineau to H. Martineau, August 7, 1859, Harriet Martineau Collection. Ibid., August 6, 1859, Item 1327.

45 Census of Great Britain 1841: Occupational Abstract, 192-99.

"others in brass and other mixed metals," and just over half the goldsmiths and jewellers. Even new trades that had appeared since 1830 depended heavily on women, children and unskilled men.[46] That a large proportion of workers in the most important industries were of such modest skill levels suggests that technological change in Birmingham was neither non-existent nor in-significant.

Although labor remained perhaps the most important cost of production (see Appendix), the supply was plentiful, relatively inexpensive, and flexible. Even initially, the Birmingham hardware industry complex did not produce the fine goods of Sheffield and thus relied less on highly skilled, highly unionized labor. According to contemporaries, at least, techno-logical changes lowered labor requirements even more.

Semi-skilled workers, on the other hand, seem to have been quite productive and to have earned relatively higher wages than elsewhere, suggesting perhaps a relative shortage. Employers did not have to pay skilled union men and employees received relatively higher wages because

---

46 J. Skirrow Wright, "An Account of Some New Trades in Birmingham, and Phases of its Social Life since 1832," _Transactions of the National Association for the Promotion of Social Science,_ 1863, 826-32.

of their productivity, although this latter observation remains highly tentative.

Thus, the hardware industry in Birmingham seemed subject to the same forces affecting the rest of industrializing Britain. Because we do not yet know enough about the impact of technological change on the labor force in Birmingham, we can conclude, based largely on contemporary evidence, only that some shifts in demand away from skilled labor toward unskilled and semi-skilled labor seem to have occurred in Birmingham, as elsewhere. Birmingham skilled workers had as much to gain or lose from technological change as workers in other major industrial cities.

Evidence inspected to this point, then, suggests that Birmingham did not clearly have a larger skilled labor component than Manchester, that Birmingham faced the same forces of change, and that the city responded in much the same way. We do not yet know precisely, however, that Birmingham necessarily had relatively less skilled labor but only that it might not have had relatively more. As a closer approximation of the historical situation we must use more refined indices to determine the importance of skilled labor realizing, of course, that even skilled labor is not a homogeneous factor of production.

Quantitatively, the next logical step involves looking at relative wage rates for similar occupations. A large supply of skilled labor, holding all other considerations fixed, would reveal itself in lower wage rates. Unfortunately, empirical problems arise immediately.

Comparing labor markets among cities involves several tasks, most basically, defining common categories, skill levels and methods of wage payment.

For Birmingham many problems appear. Wage data are scattered, rarely systematic, and generally inadequate either in time or numbers covered. Day wage data for agricultural workers and other traditional workers, like building craftsmen, exist, but in the newer industries piece-work remained the rule, and occupational classifications changed rapidly. Because of the social and political problems they caused, factories in the North and the East Midlands came under much scrutiny, and as a result reasonably good wage data and job descriptions exist. Birmingham hardwares never received such exhaustive coverage and the incredibly varied production processes, each with its own highly fluctuating piece-rates, make wage comparability tenuous at best. Because of their small size, few firms retained records.

Nonetheless, an examination of wage rates, even from such partial data, can lead to useful insights about the nature and composition of the labor market, as long as we exercise appropriate restraint in generalizing.

Wages

Because firm income data for the industrial revolution do not exist, we must rely on wages for basic statistical sustenance. Overall wage rates changed little nationally in the first half of the 19th century. Mitchell and Deane record only about a ten percent increase in the index of wages of shipbuilders and engineers from 1810 to 1853, while compositors slipped slightly and building remained quite constant.[47] In a broad sense, average wages for mechanical trades and metal workers throughout England seemed to fall within the 20s. to 40s. band cited earlier.

Some indices suggest that Birmingham skilled labor received less than skilled labor in other areas. The heavy edge tool trade that one observor claimed moved to Birmingham about mid-century to escape the controls of Sheffield unions seems not to have paid extraordinarily well in its new location. Despite partial wage data, even more patterns emerge. For example,

---

47 B. R. Mitchell, P. Deane, Abstract of British Historical Statistics, Cambridge University Press, 1962, 349.

skilled workers, like forgers and grinders in the edge tool industry, earned more in Sheffield than in Wolverhampton:

Occupation	Shillings per week		
	1840	1850	1860
Edge tool forgers			
Sheffield	29	32s.6d.	36
Wolverhampton	30	30	30
Edge tool grinders			
Sheffield	34	36	38
Wolverhampton	25-30	25-30	25-30

Sources: Sheffield figures from Board of Trade, Returns of Wages published between 1830 and 1886, 191. Wolverhampton figures from Ibid., 197.

Because of their proximity, Wolverhampton and and Birmingham shared the same labor market. Even allowing for some incomparability, the differential between Sheffield and Wolverhampton remains significant.

The shift of locations that Timmins cited probably allowed manufacturers to substitute labor-saving machinery like tilt hammers, squeezers, shears, and rollers.[48] It is

---

48 S. Timmins, ed., Birmingham and the Midlands Hardware District, 1866, A. Kelley, New York, 1968, 657.

important to remain aware of uncertainties caused by the data. Wage-earners were not easily distinguished from subcontractors. Thus, observors labelled "workmen" those who hired others to help them make complete metal components, and wages over about 40s. a week probably covered the cost of an assistant or apprentice. For example, workers who made and assembled all parts earned only 25s. to 35s. a week, but 40s. to 80s. a week with help. Dippers and bronzers who did only specialized tasks in the gas fittings trade earned from 20s. to 25s. a week.[49] Of particular value was an apprentice, especially "towards the close of his term," whose wages fell well below his marginal revenue product.[50]

Indirect evidence suggests that wages for many skilled workers were in the 20s. to 25s. range, and piece rates made earnings even more variable. In the prosperous Birmingham gunmaking industry in 1866, for example, adult male gun barrel filers earned from 15s. to 40s. a week, a tremendous range. Gun finishers

---

49 Ibid., 353.

50 W. Ryland, "The Plated Wares and Electroplating Trades", S. Timmins, ed., Birmingham and the Midlands Hardware District, 1866, 479.

and rib forgers fell within the same range, and perhaps the most consistently highly paid workers, gun machiners, earned 30s. to 36s. a week. Gun barrel browners had the widest range, from 20s. to 60s., presumably depending on the number of assistants or apprentices.[51]

Despite the variety of occupations, the existence of piece rates, and the incomparability of many occupations among cities, some generalizations seem warranted. First, in Birmingham as in the other major industrial cities, hierarchies of earnings existed among and within mechanical trades (ignoring for the moment building, domestic, and distributive trades). "Skilled" workers earned 20s. to 40s. a week by themselves.

Second, despite great ranges in many of the most important trades, average earnings seemed to fall between 20s. and 25s. a week. The average 24s.3d. for men mechanics cited by the survey in 1840 seems corroborated by contemporaries and studies by the Board of Trade in the latter part of the century.

Third, wages for many Birmingham skilled workers seem to have been less than those for similar workers in other cities. Indirect and

---

[51] Board of Trade, Returns 1830-1886, 199.

direct evidence seems to support this contention. In any case, it does not seem that skilled workers in Birmingham were in much better condition than their colleagues in other areas. In jobs unique to hardware operations Birmingham employees who received skilled workers wages were in the lower quarter of wages for skilled workers nationally. To draw a more complete comparison of Birmingham with Manchester, it is useful to look at wages in jobs common in both cities and in both industries.

Although job classifications differed widely among industries, some jobs were basic throughout all industries during and after the industrial revolution. Among the few categories in this group are millwrights, blacksmiths, carpenters, patternmakers, and other types of fabricators and mechanics. By comparing rates for these skills, a clearer picture of relative wages will emerge.

Roughly the same provisos applicable to the mechanical trades also apply here. Even for the same job classification, wages could vary according to industry. Thus, in Manchester laborers in wire working earned slightly more than laborers in engineering works from 1839 to 1859.[52]

---

[52] D. Chadwick, "On the Rate of Wages", 25.

Among the most common trades, Birmingham clearly fell below going rates in many areas, as the following table and graphs attest:

Occupation	1839 Manch.	1839 Bm.[2]	1849 M.	1849 B.[3]	1859 M.	1859 B.[4]
	Shillings/Week					
Smiths	30	21	32	18	32	22
Boilermakers[1]	22	18	30	18	32	16
Fitters[1]	30	24	30	22	32	21
Foundrymen	30	21	34	20	34	23
Patternmakers	30	23	30	24	32	25
Laborers[1]	16	23	15	24	16	18

[1] in engineering works (Manchester data from Chadwick "On the Rate of Wages", 25.)

[2] average payrolls for April 29, 1837 and November 11, 1837. Spring and Fall months chosen to average effects of seasonal employment. (My calculation). Boulton and Watt Collection, Weekly Wages and Extras, Box 559, Birmingham Reference Library.

[3] average payrolls for April 4, 1846 and November 14, 1846.

[4] average payrolls for April 28, 1866 and November 24, 1866.

Note: 1839, 1849, 1859 Boulton and Watt data not available at time of writing.

Chadwick excluded young persons except in trades where they were important. Chadwick, "On the Rate of Wages," 3. The Boulton and Watt data do not disclose whether boys are included. Boys were included explicitly in the Boulton and Watt data later in the century, although they were not segregated from men in total wage figures.

WEEKLY WAGES FOR SELECTED OCCUPATIONS IN BIRMINGHAM AND MANCHESTER, 1839-59

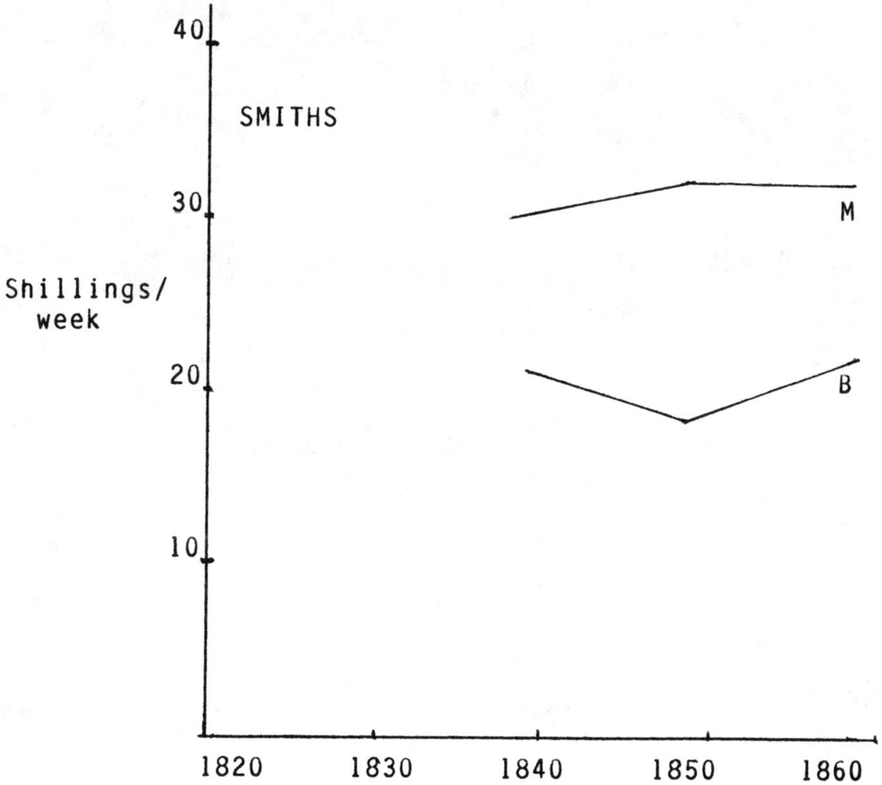

WEEKLY WAGES FOR SELECTED OCCUPATIONS IN BIRMINGHAM AND MANCHESTER, 1839-59

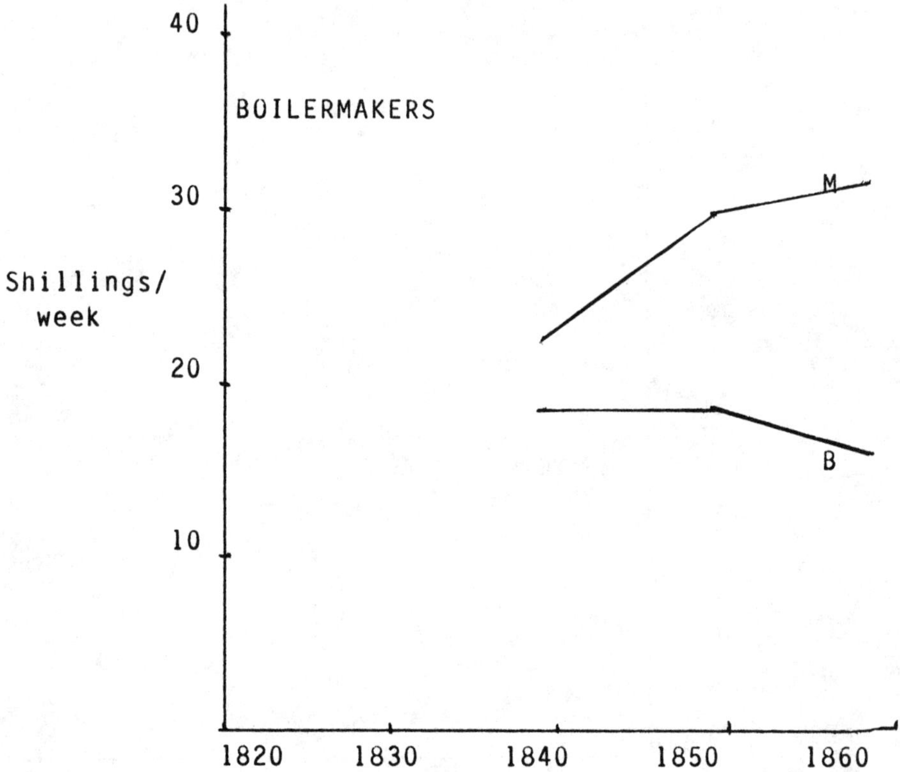

WEEKLY WAGES FOR SELECTED OCCUPATIONS IN BIRMINGHAM AND MANCHESTER, 1839-59

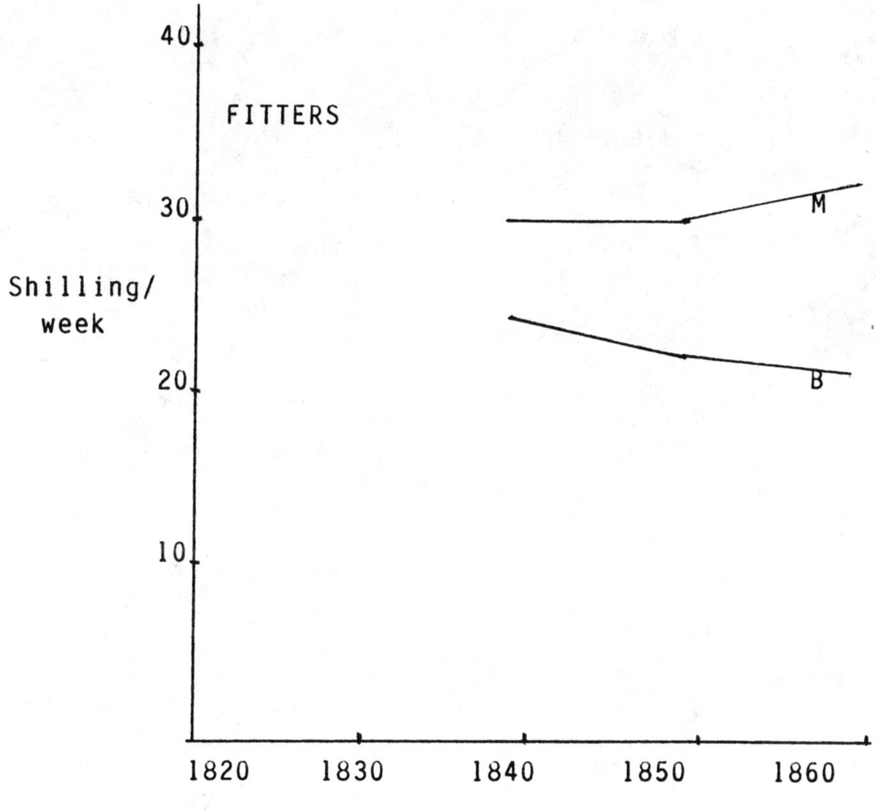

WEEKLY WAGES FOR SELECTED OCCUPATIONS IN BIRMINGHAM AND MANCHESTER, 1839-59

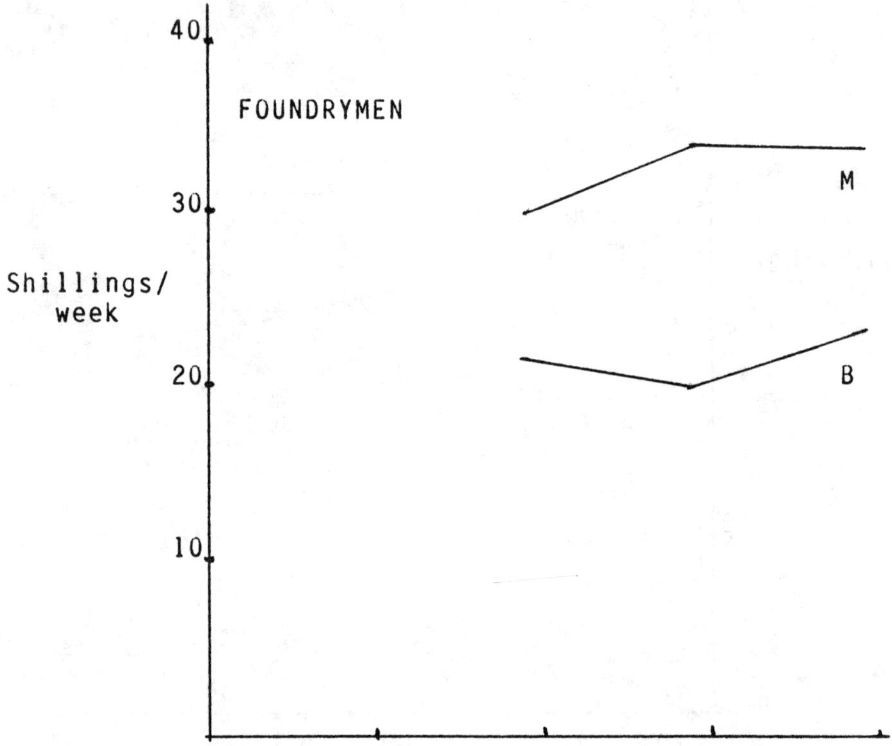

WEEKLY WAGES FOR SELECTED OCCUPATIONS IN BIRMINGHAM AND MANCHESTER, 1839-59

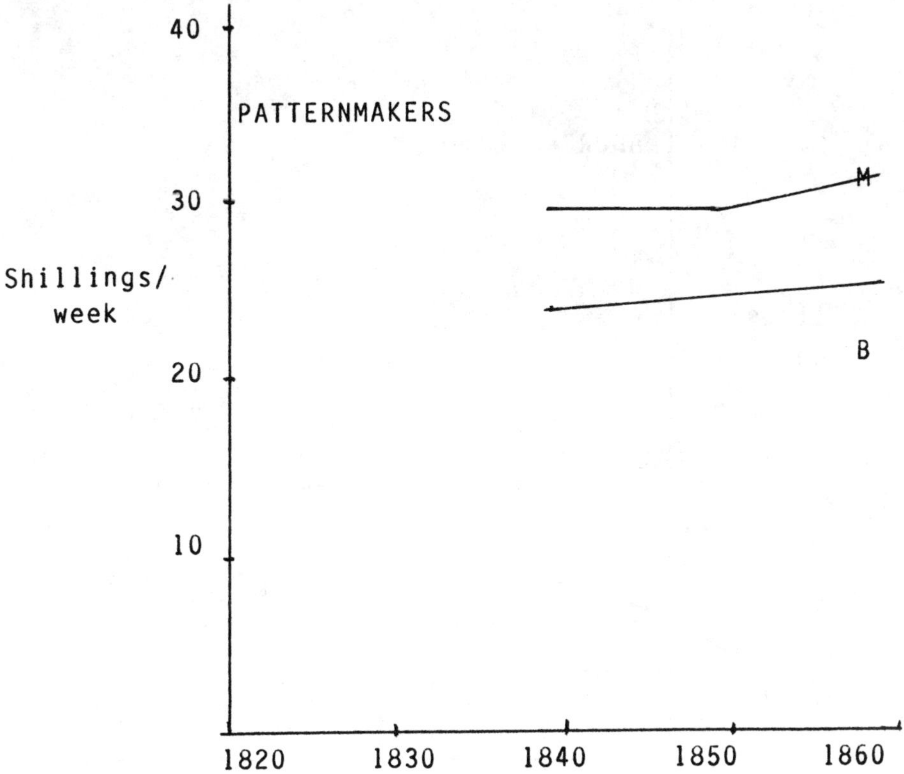

WEEKLY WAGES FOR SELECTED OCCUPATIONS IN BIRMINGHAM AND MANCHESTER, 1839-59

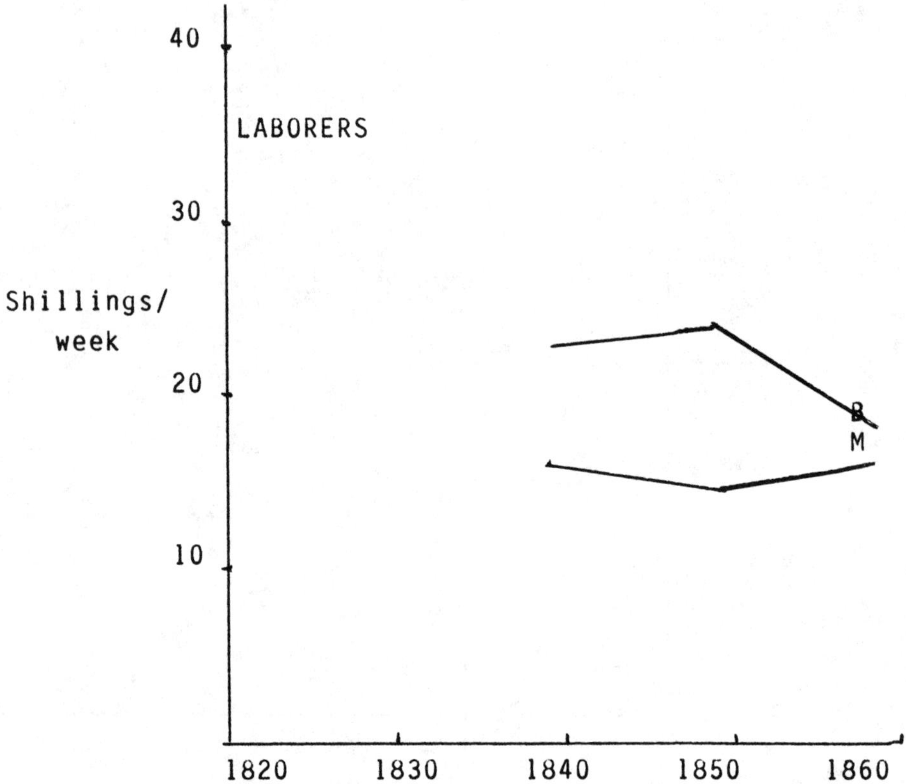

The differences are striking. Birmingham skilled workers received much less on average than Manchester men, but Birmingham laborers fared much better. In Birmingham, wage levels for such unskilled and semiskilled labor seem often to have reached those of skilled men.

The relatively higher wage rates for skilled workers in Manchester suggests a scarcity there, while the relatively lower wage rates for laborers suggests a surplus. This finding seems to contradict earlier observations based on the data concerning the percentage of men in the workforce and the skilled-labor displacing thrust of technological change in Birmingham. (One must recall that these wage data apply only to well-defined skills common to both industries rather than skills unique to either. Conclusions regarding the latter might differ.)

Several explanations for this apparent incompatibility seem possible:

One, because we do not yet have a fully operational system of defining or identifying skilled labor, the methods used thus far bear refinement. Because we also lack an operational measure of the impact of technological change on the labor force, we have no precise awareness of the dimensions involved and must accept qualitative data, such as observations by contemporaries, as applying to some members of the workforce but not many. Thus, Birmingham might have had relatively more skilled workers, although they would not have been relatively better off economically as the traditional interpretation suggested.[53]

Two, moving from a strictly market to a more institutional view, the Birmingham hardware industries might have employed relatively fewer skilled workers and have paid them less because of the inability or reluctance of workers to organize into trade unions. Ironically, the very lack of trade unions suggests either that most workers had few skills to monopolize and protect, or that the prevalence of piece rates stymied skilled workers from organizing. Although scholars have hardly reached consensus on the ability of unions to raise wages, many contemporaries believed that they could, and, in any case, an investigation of this relationship offers a way to explain apparently lower wage rates in Birmingham.[54]

---

53 Briggs, Victorian Cities, 186.

54 For discussions of unions and wage change see, for example, R. Perlman, editor, Wage Determination: Market or Power Forces, D. C. Heath and Co., Lexington, Massachusetts, 1964.

Trade Unions

Contemporaries considered low wages in Birmingham an established fact. According to William Ryland in the 1860s relatively low wages in the plating trade were an important asset to Birmingham manufacturers. Wages failed to rise above competitive levels not only because of close identification of men with masters in the small workshops but also because the piece rate system offered no common focusses for resentment. Piece rates changed with shifts in demand for the diverse output. Working at different rates making different products, men could not easily concentrate on a single wage target or set of targets, causing most attempts at combination to die stillborn.[55]

Men earned as much as their skill and endurance would allow in a highly competitive labor market. Wages for the same type work varied from 22s. to 40s. a week in day men's wages in the plating trade, with most workers probably earning wages nearer the lower bound. Similarly, the typical man in the metallic pen making trade earned 18s. to 20s. a week, although "the skilled [faster working?]adult

---

55 Ryland, "The Plated Wares," 479.

makes from 30s. to 80s., and some even 90s. and 100s. per week".[56]

Workers rarely confronted employers head on in Birmingham, which generally avoided much of the strife that plagued much of Britain, especially during the 1830s and 1840s. Even the Chartist movement had relatively little impact.[57]

Several reasons might explain such relative passivity. The traditional workshop structure of the major industries meant a relatively low number of employees per employer, often under 30 workers per firm.[58] Even though Sheffield had basically the same form of industry, the city was very tightly organized, perhaps because the greater skills needed for the city's fine work made for more cohesion.[59] Adam Smith

---

56 Timmins, Birmingham and the Midlands Hardware District, 636.

57 T. Tholfsen, "The Chartist Crisis in Birmingham," International Review of Social History, 1958, 461-80.

58 A. Briggs, "Thomas Attwood and the Economic Background of the Birmingham Political Union," Cambridge Historical Journal, 1948, 199. In 1843 the Commission of Child Labor gave average size as six to thirty workers.

59 As Harrison noted for London, relatively few skilled workers were organized in trade unions and these made fine wares almost exclusively. Harrison, The Early Victorians, 24.

noted ruefully the power of privileged trades to restrict output and employment in Sheffield compared with both Manchester and Birmingham.[60] Citing another study, David Landes stressed that probably fewer than one-fifth of all Birmingham apprentices had served their time fully, suggesting negligible control over the labor market.[61]

Samuel Timmins (as a Birmingham manufacturer, not a wholly disinterested observor) remarked that the heavy edge tool trade moved from Sheffield to Birmingham in the early 19th century because of the "unwillingness" of workers (read: resistance to technological unemployment) to try new techniques.[62] Another manufacturer, William Ryland, credited piece-work with holding down strike activity because the "great variety of patterns and the multiplicity of the parts of which many of the articles were composed. . . ." required individual bargaining for each piece of work, which presumably benefited masters more than

---

60 Adam Smith, The Wealth of Nations, 1776, E. Cannan, ed., Modern Library, New York, 119.

61 D. Landes, Unbound Prometheus, 62n, citing Chevalier, "La Mission de Gabriel Jars," Transactions of the Newcomen Society, XXVI (1947/8 and 1948/9), 63.

62 Timmins, Birmingham and the Midlands Hardware District, 656.

men.[63] As paeans to Birmingham workers in Timmins' collection attested, manufacturers found the city highly attractive for its docile labor force. Indeed, as late as 1859 workmen had such little control over their jobs that a Birmingham employer could recall only two strikes in his time.[64] A year later the National Association for the Promotion of Social Science published a thick volume on Trades' Societies and Strikes, hardly mentioning Birmingham.[65]

If partial wage data only hint at lower wages, employers like Timmins knew very well why manufacturers set up in Birmingham. Piece rates not only held down wages but also slowed trade union growth, which meant no work rules and few if any strikes. In a study of trade union strength in various counties in England and South Wales, Sidney and Beatrice Webb rated Birmingham quite low. In Birmingham only 4.1 percent of the population were trade union members, compared with Northumberland,

---

[63] Ryland, "The Plated Wares," 479.

[64] R. F. Martineau to H. Martineau, August 7, 1859, Harriet Martineau Collection, HM 1321, University of Birmingham.

[65] National Association for Promotion of Social Science, Trades' Societies and Strikes, London, 1860, reprinted by A. M. Kelley, New York, 1968.

which ranked highest, with relatively almost three times as many.[66]

The variegated shop environment has often seemed to cloud analysis but despite this welter of workshops, Alan Fox discerned a basic job structure to industry in Birmingham that bore directly on labor relations. Although few large factories existed, individual entrepreneurs built much economic power by becoming factors, who coordinated production and supplied working capital to workshops (with up to 50 employees each), or by becoming employers, who took subcontractors under their roofs and provided them with power and other essentials for fees. In either case, the factor or employer paid piece rates to the workshop owner or subcontractor, who in turn paid day rates to his own hands.[67] The hands themselves generally worked at very specialized

---

[66] As Fox had rightly pointed out, traditional explanations for such weakness in a major industrial city have borne little scrutiny. Close relations between masters and men do not guarantee good relations, and as the Sheffield experience shows, unions can flourish even in small workshops. Yet, Birmingham did not mature in union development until much later in the century, and remained an amenable environment for employers even in the 1860s. Alan Fox, "Industrial Relations in Nineteenth Century Birmingham," Oxford Economic Papers,1955,58.

[67] Ibid., 58-9. See also Livesay and Porter, cited in Chapter Three of the present study.

unskilled or semiskilled tasks, and rarely acquired all the skills of the particular trade. As noted, no comprehensive apprenticeship system existed.[68]

Naturally, boys easily filled many jobs, and could earn quite good sums, relatively, until their late teens, when employers found it more profitable to dismiss them in favor of younger hands.[69]

Not surprisingly, subcontractors rather than hands created the first trade associations in the 1870s, and found ready support from the biggest employers, who hoped that high prices would destroy the small garret-masters, who easily entered the trades and caused ferocious competition.[70] Subcontractors could hardly threaten to strike with such a reserve of small, eager producers, and could not rely on public opinion either, since they were generally quite amply situated. Logically, they allied with the most substantial employers to force prices up and competition out.[71] Indeed, not until technological and organizational change had reorganized the industrial structure of the city did day workers become the majority

---

[68] _Ibid_., 59-60.

[69] _Ibid_.

[70] _Ibid_., 62-3.

[71] _Ibid_., 63-5.

voice in trade associations. By then semi-skilled machine operators had grown far more important to the production process than the old skilled craftsmen.[72]

Thus, the semi-independence of the subcontractors, the enormous variety of goods they produced, their own positions as employers, and the lack of trade union tradition forestalled trade union development for the better part of a century.

Of course, many artisans worked for subcontractors, but entry into light metal trades, at however low a level, came relatively easily and with some effort a workman could become a small master himself, taking on all the attitudes and status that such a position implied, according to one historian.[73]

Identifying strongly with middle-class desires and aspirations, Birmingham artisans were said to have been a key component of the well integrated social and political culture of the city, reducing employer-employee abrasions or at least neutralizing them.[74]

Politically, such cohesion placed

---

72 Ibid., 68.

73 T. Tholfsen, "The Artisan and Culture of Early Victorian Birmingham," University of Birmingham Historical Journal, 1953-4, 151.

74 Ibid., 165.

Birmingham in a far different position from other major urban-industrial centers. In the excited years before the passage of the Reform Bill in 1832, for example, political activists in Birmingham stood behind Thomas Attwood, whose scheme to increase currency to relieve unemployment united masters and men alike.[75] Unlike Birmingham employers, who sought high prices, Manchester manufacturers primarily wanted low costs and thus concentrated on eliminating the Corn Laws.[76]

Employers and employees in Leeds also divided: the former, interested mainly in parliamentary reform to enfranchise more householders; the latter, concerned with ameliorating problems of rapid technological change.[77]

An outgrowth of the wild economic fluctuations that had beset the city since the second decade of the century, the Birmingham Political Union, founded by Attwood and fifteen others

---

75 A. Briggs, "The Background of the Parliamentary Reform Movement in Three English Cities (1830-2)," Cambridge Historical Journal, 1952, 298.

76 Ibid., 305.

77 Ibid., 310.

in late 1829, sought to unite all sections of the populace for economic reform.[78] As the crowd of 12,000 to 15,000 that heard the reading of the rules attested, the unification largely succeeded.[79] Within the Political Union Attwood's currency supporters held sway, assuring cohesion against common enemies: Parliament and especially the Bank of England.[80]

Little interested in repealing the Corn Laws, and therefore supported by some landowners, Attwood argued directly against the theory of Ricardo and the "Manchester School" that an automatic system of full employment existed.[81] He wanted to break the bond between currency and gold and require the Bank of England to issue currency whenever unemployment began to rise.[82] Insistent that "the first and most important duty for the Legislature to attend to, is to take care that an ample demand for labour is restored and maintained throughout the country," Attwood urged the government to

---

78 A. Briggs, "Thomas Attwood and the Economic Background of the Birmingham Political Union," Cambridge Historical Journal, 1948, 210-1.

79 Ibid., 211

80 Ibid., 191, 205.

81 S. G. Checkland, "The Birmingham Economists, 1815-1850," Economic History Review, 1948, 2.

82 Ibid., 8; Briggs, "Thomas Attwood", 205.

increase prices vastly during times of distress by inflating the currency.[83] He gained even more support from lower income groups by advocating unbalanced budgets, and sumptuary and property taxes.[84]

Except for a brief period in the late 1830s and early 1840s, Birmingham masters and men worked together against the threat of unemployment caused by slack demand.[85]

Indeed, Birmingham workers reacted with such relative calm to the Chartists that an investigation of the movement devoted entire chapters to Wales, Manchester, and Glasgow, and to the lesser areas of Leicester, Leeds, and Suffolk, while only infrequently nodding to Birmingham.[86] Lack of organized strength seems best explained by market rather than political conditions, however. Without many skills to monopolize, and finding employers embracing full employment rather than cost reduction, Birmingham workers seemed to have had little trouble identifying with their masters.

---

83 Thomas Attwood letter to Robert Peel in Aris's Birmingham Gazette, Jan. 30, 1843, as found in F. W. Fetter, ed., Selected Economic Writings of Thomas Attwood, London School of Economics, 1964, 17.

84 Checkland, "The Birmingham Economists," 15.

85 T. Tholfsen, "The Chartist Crisis in Birmingham," 461-80.

86 A. Briggs, ed., Chartist Studies, MacMillan, London, 195

Thus, we still cannot quite accept the view that skilled labor was relatively abundant in Birmingham because evidence regarding trade union weakness adds to the interdeterminate nature of answers reached to this point.

Another area of investigation remains open, however: the issue of employment and income stability. If, for example, Birmingham offered both entrepreneurs and skilled workers relatively stable income, even though based on lower profits and wages, the city would have attracted a highly talented, inexpensive citizenry. Such hypothesized stability would also help explain the lack of social tension and trade unions. Unfortunately,Birmingham proved as luckless as its sister industrial cities in providing such a secure environment.

Employment and Income Stability

One can view employment stability from two perspectives: the employer finds his labor force stable when he can get as many workers as he needs; the employee finds work stable when he can find jobs whenever he needs them. The two phenomena do not necessarily exist concurrently.

To state, as earlier historians have done, that stable employment must exist because workers can easily shift jobs due to a common denominator of skills is to hope for employment rather than to realize it. Possession of skill does not guarantee employment in either short or long run. No evidence proves the existence of ready employment in Birmingham, but much suggests the opposite. Indeed, employment stability must be considered part of the broader issue of standard of living to make meaningful distinctions between cities.

Despite the duration and intensity of the standard of living debate between "optimists" and"pessimists" few firm conclusions have resulted, partly because antagonists have used overaggregated data. Although no microscopic studies of Birmingham itself exist, G. J. Barnsby's analysis of the Black Country offers much insight.[87]

Although Birmingham prospered throughout much of the Napoleonic war period, a sharp depression in 1811 sent over 9,000 inhabitants, over ten percent of the population, to poor

---

87 G. J. Barnsby, "Standard of Living in the Black Country," Economic History Review, May, 1971. See also R. S. Neale, "Standard of Living, 1780-1844: Regional and Class Study," Economic History Review, 1966.

relief.[88] Trade picked up during the teens but another severe downswing occurred in 1819, and the numbers on poor relief swelled gradually in the twenties and early thirties to a peak in 1833 of over 10,000. (see graph) The numbers declined during the rest of the thirties, but such fluctuations continued into the mid-Victorian period. Among pieceworkers short-time work was the worst problem in the Black Country, and, given the similarity between Birmingham and the Black Country in many industries and jobs, presumably the same held true in Birmingham.[89]

From 1815 to 1900, Barnsby found only 23 years of full employment in the Black Country, most of them widely dispersed, except in 1834-7, 1845-55, and 1870-4.[90] Workers simply shared the limited piecework available.[91] Of the five major trades studied by Barnsby (miners, engineers, iron, construction, and domestic hardware workers), all but miners and primary iron workers played considerable roles in the Birmingham labor force.

Throughout the period, engineers earned fairly stable wages and building trades workers

---

[88] A. Briggs, "Thomas Attwood", 195.; W. L. Sargant, "On the Vital Statistics of Birmingham and Seven Other Large Towns," Journal of the Statistical Society, March 1866, 102.

[89] Briggs, "Thomas Attwood," 197.; "Contributions to the Economical Statistics of Birmingham," 439.

[90] Barnsby, "Standard of Living in the Black Country," 22.

[91] *Ibid.*, 223, 221.

NUMBER OF PERSONS ON POOR RELIEF IN BIRMINGHAM

1820 - 39

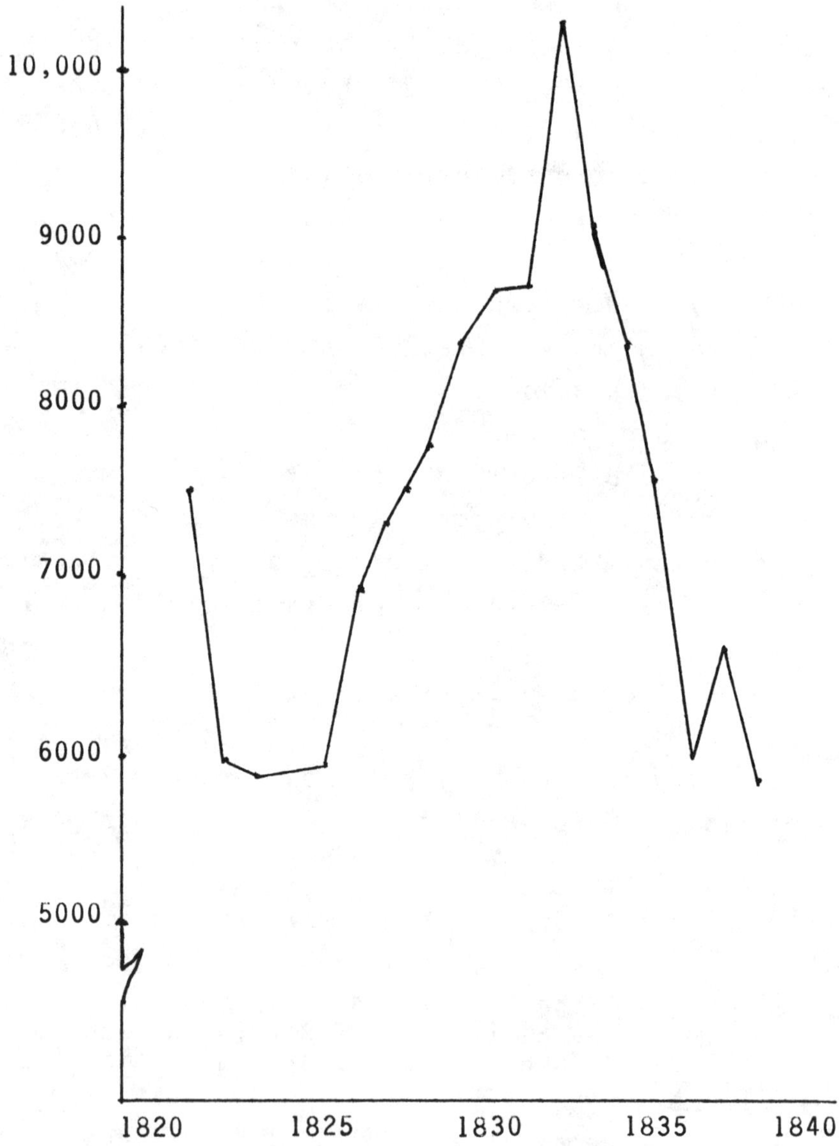

Source: "Economical Statistics of Birmingham," Journal of the Statisitcal Society, 1840, 439.

actually increased their earnings. Terribly sensitive to economic fluctuation, domestic workers suffered most. Adult male domestic workers in nail, lock, chain, and key making earned between 7s. and 20s. a week, and generally attained the latter only infrequently.[92]

Suffering from such wild earnings gyrations, domestic workers often lived at the margin of survival.[93] Devising estimates of minimum standards of subsistence and minimum standards of comfort, Barnsby found 25 percent of the Black Country population living above a minimum standard of comfort, 20 percent below a minimum standard of subsistence, and the remainder between these upper and lower bounds, with proportions changing little over time.[94]

---

[92] Ibid., 223.

[93] Ibid., 224.

[94] Ibid., 223. Minimum standard of comfort was twice the minimum standard of subsistence. For a family of parents and two small children, the minimum standard of comfort was a family income of 29s 3d. in 1840, 25s. in 1850, and 28s. in 1860. He does not explain how 20 percent of the population could live below subsistence. Presumably, these are averages and might not hold for an individual family for long (i.e., a family might have moved in and out of such a position.)

Sharp, short, trade fluctuations threatened Birmingham workers and small entrepreneurs constantly and shredded financial security. Like other industrial centers, Birmingham suffered dearly from gouges in prosperity. Writing in the 1790s, F. M. Eden estimated that one-fifteenth to one-twelfth of the population received poor relief.[95] Poor relief soared from £21,000 in 1811 to £33,000 one year later and to £42,000 in 1813. Payments dropped somewhat but then climbed sharply to £62,000 in 1818. Throughout the early 19th century such severe fluctuations remained common, as the following graph suggests.[96]

---

95 F. M. Eden, State of the Poor, Vol. III, +738. See also lists of the poor and outpoor, extant for 1776, 1781, 1784, 1789 (probably the same as 1790), and 1822 and the Birmingham parish poor rate levy books for much of the 18th and 19th centuries in the Birmingham Reference Library. Local newspapers regularly carried lists of bankrupts usually taken from London papers.

96 Jaffray, Hints, Ch. 44.

AMOUNT SPENT ON POOR RELIEF IN BIRMINGHAM

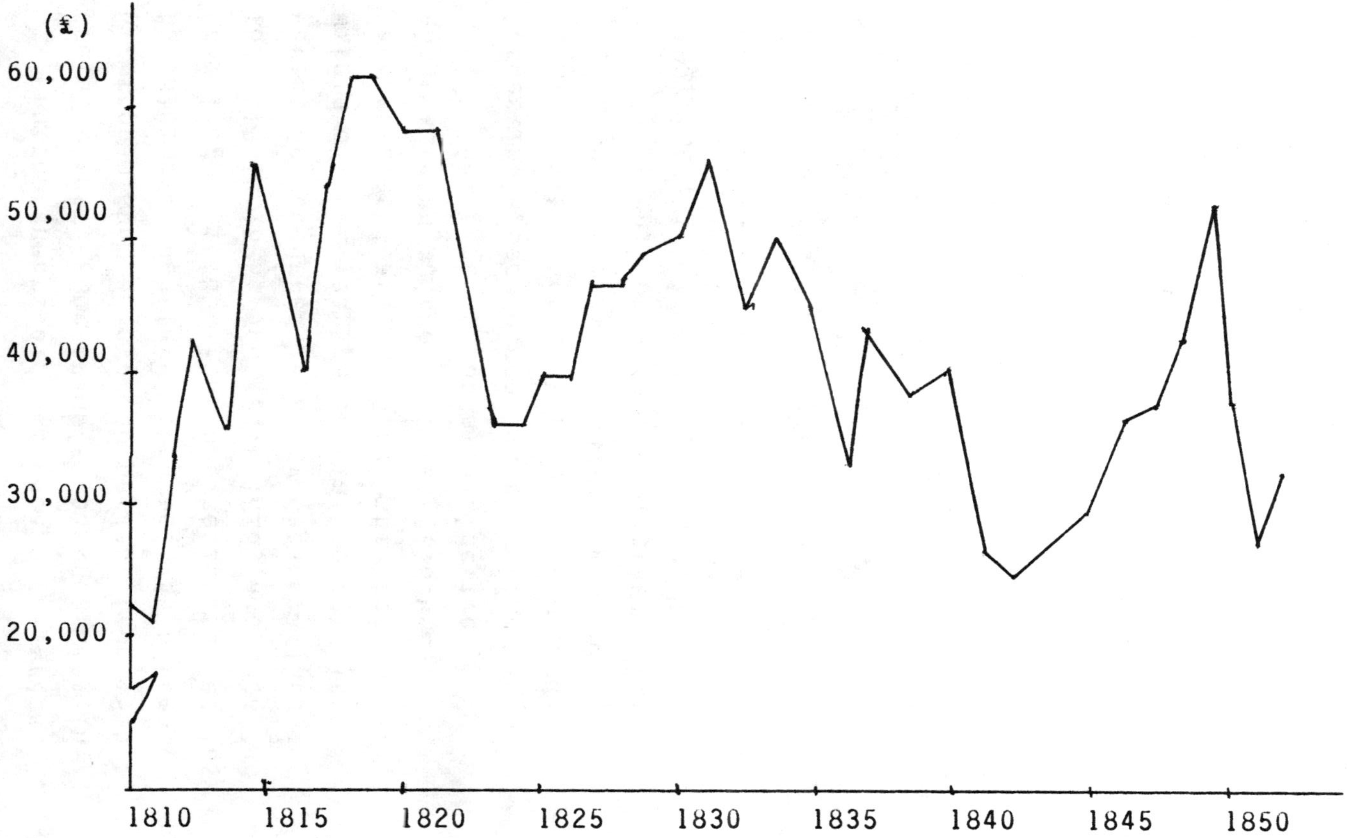

Source: Jaffray, Hints, Ch.44.

Entrepreneurs did not escape the trade cycle, either. For example, bankruptcies in Birmingham shot up over 50 percent from 1815 to 1816, remained level then fell 50 percent from 1817 to 1818. Four businesses failed in 1824, 19 in 1825, and 49 in 1826, and such variations occurred in every decade. Thus, within a three year period in the thirties bankruptcies nearly tripled, then fell by about a third in the last year (1836-8).[97]

Economic recession hit selectively. Suggesting a secure constituency, the Birmingham Savings Bank slipped in deposit growth only four times and in number of depositors only once in its first 24 years (1827-1850).[98]

---

97 Ibid., Ch. 50.

98 Ibid., Ch. 33

Summary and Conclusions

Although most data are poor and generate more questions than answers, some impressions about the labor force in Birmingham hardwares seem defensible. We cannot unequivocally attribute to Birmingham the three traits devised by some contemporaries and historians discussed in this chapter: prevalence of skilled labor, slowness of technological change, and capacity to withstand trade fluctuations.

Semi-skilled and unskilled labor, performed by women, children, and adult males, represented the majority of workers and seemed to grow increasingly valuable as the industrial revolution in Birmingham progressed. One cannot yet safely argue that small, skill-intensive workshops became anachronistic by the middle of the nineteenth century, but certainly technology using unskilled and semi-skilled labor grew more important.

Because of its small scale, cumulative nature technological change in Birmingham has suffered severe underestimation. R. B. Prosser tallied the number of patents granted Birmingham inventors but observors have tended either to ignore him or discuss only descriptively the inventions themselves. As yet, no one has undertaken a systematic analysis of the impact of technological change on employment in workshop industries in Birmingham.[99]

The sheer fact that changes did occur in Birmingham during the industrial revolution help explain why the city had no natural, unique resistance to economic instability. Affected by all national downswings as well as declines in specific hardware trades, Birmingham did not remain an island of relative comfort but suffered, as all full participants did, in the gyrations of industrial activity of the late 18th and early 19th centuries.

Tied closely to output by piece-rates, hardware workers lost income or jobs quickly when demand for goods fell, much like industrial workers everywhere in Britain. One cannot safely argue that employment was stable simply because skills were transferable. Skills mean nothing without jobs and job opportunities are determined by a variety of factors.

---

99 For a partial exception see N. Rosenberg, The American System of Manufactures, Edinburgh University Press, 1969, 1-89, passim.

One major area remains to be investigated, however. A system of skilled labor, no matter how pervasive, must rely on institutions to preserve the trades, or at least on flows of already trained workers into the trades; that is, without either extensive immigration or training systems, skilled arts must gradually decline. The existence of widespread immigration of skilled workers or comprehensive training systems would clearly indicate the prevalence of skilled labor in Birmingham. We must turn then to such an inspection.

CHAPTER FIVE: SOURCES OF LABOR, TRAINING, AND EDUCATION

Sources of Labor

The frequency and severity of short-time work and the steady growth of the population of the city in the early 19th century suggests an ample supply of labor of all skills. Throughout England the close of the Napoleonic wars ushered in several decades of overfull labor markets at many times in many places and Birmingham proved no exception.

With peak years during the teens (18 percent growth) and the seventies (14 percent), the population of England and Wales increased at around two million persons a decade throughout much of the 19th century, from 10 million in 1811 to 23 million in 1871.[1]

Population growth in provincial centers and in the north peaked in the twenties when Liverpool, Manchester, Birmingham, Leeds, Sheffield, Bradford, and Salford grew 40 to 45 percent.[2] (See graph) During the next

---

1 S. G. Checkland, The Rise of Industrial Society in England 1815-1885, Longmans, London, 1964, 27, 28.

2 Ibid., 238.

decade, however, all but Liverpool and Bradford slackened, although towns greater than 20,000 grew faster than England as a whole.[3] Although Birmingham sustained the 27 percent growth of the thirties, other large towns fell during the forties: Wolverhampton from 38 to 28 percent, Leeds from 23 to 13 percent, Liverpool from 42 to 31 percent, and Bristol from 20 to 10 percent.[4] During the fifties, Birmingham continued to grow at 27 percent a decade, Sheffield shot up from 22 to 37 percent, and Leeds from 13 to 20 percent, but Manchester fell sharply from 30 to 13 percent and Liverpool from 31 to 18 percent.[5]

Overall, during the first 60 years of the 19th century, the cotton textile towns (Manchester, Liverpool, and Leeds), broadly defined, generally increased more rapidly than the hard-

---

[3] Ibid., 239.

[4] Sargent, "Vital Statistics," 102-3.

[5] Using different statistics, Checkland suggests that hardware towns grew more rapidly than textile towns during the forties. Checkland, 239. There are two problems with this generalization: first, the figures he used applied to Registrar districts rather than to more natural boundaries, Sargant, "Vital Statistics," 104, 94 and second he does not note that Wolverhampton declined during the period and that Manchester remained steady, using the more natural borough rather than registration (Poor Law Board) boundaries. Sargant, "Vital Statistics," 102-3, 94.

ware towns (Birmingham, Wolverhampton, and Sheffield), although both groups increased much faster than England and Wales in general and London in particular. Birmingham grew 4.19 times, Wolverhampton 4.82, and Sheffield 4.05; but Liverpool leapt forward 5.40 times, Manchester 4.66, and Leeds, a laggard, 3.90.[6]

Only inadequate data suggest the sources of the new population, for earlier studies used the county rather than the city as the unit of investigation. Birmingham created particular problems because of its location at the corner of three counties, leading to overestimation of the impact of intercounty migration. Using admittedly crude data, however, one can draw a rough sketch of demographic change.

Of the inhabitants of Warwickshire, nearly 70 percent were natives, and just over nine percent came from neighboring (i.e., close to Birmingham) Staffordshire and Worcestershire. The next largest group came not from a contiguous county, but from Ireland, which supplied two-and-one-half

---

[6] *Ibid.*, 102-3.

POPULATION GROWTH IN BIRMINGHAM, MANCHESTER
SHEFFIELD, 1801-1861

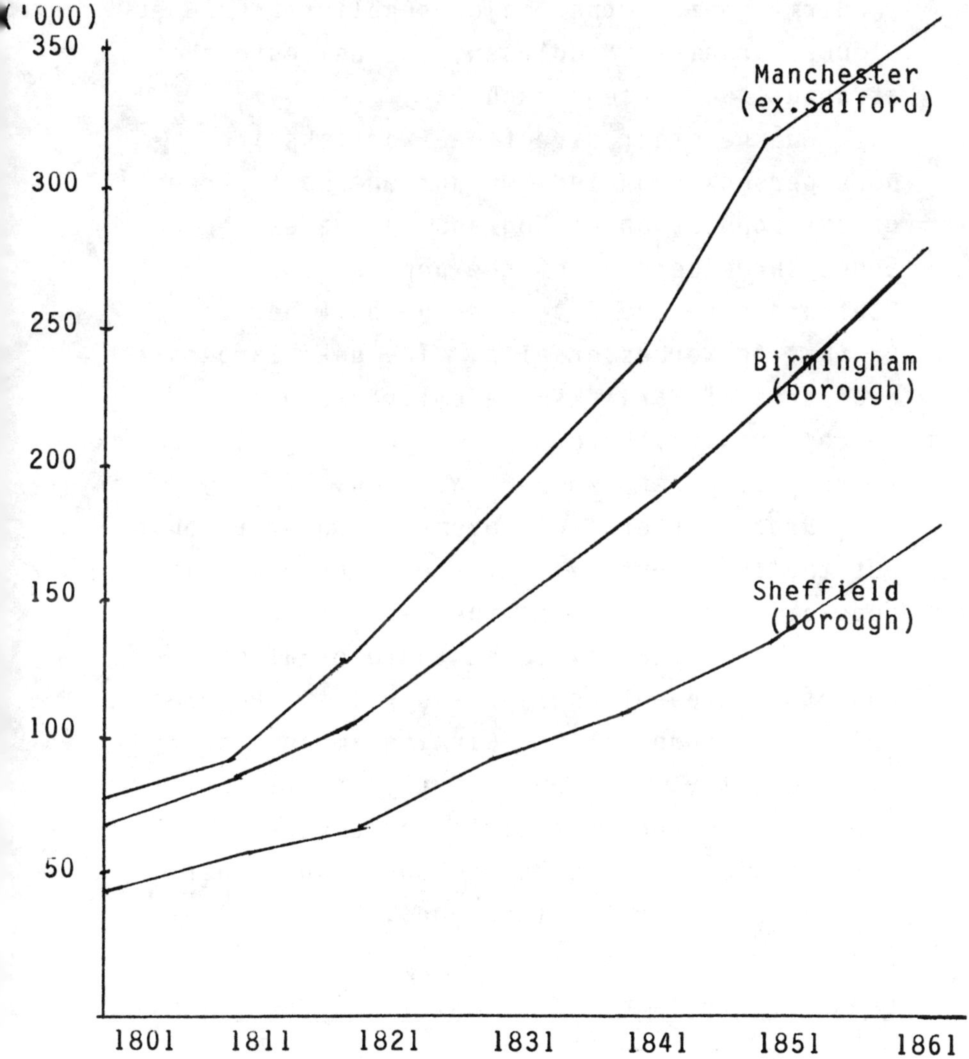

Source: Sargant, "Vital Statistics," JSS, 1866, 102-3.

percent of the population of the county and presumably a much higher percentage of that in Birmingham. Other major suppliers included Gloucestershire, Middlesex, and Leicestershire, at about two percent each.[7]

On the other direction, Warwickshire-born persons supplied two-and-one-half percent of the population of England and Wales, but about three percent of the population in Staffordshire and five-and-one-half percent of that in Worcestershire. The next largest recipents of Warwickshire emigrants were Leicestershire, Oxfordshire, and Northhamptonshire, all under two percent each.[8]

Broad patterns of movement appear throughout the 19th century. R. Lawton argued that population movements in the West Midlands from 1841 to 1861 exceeded those of almost any other area of England and Wales. People left rural counties for Birmingham and the Black Country, but concurrently others left the West Midlands for South Lancashire, Western Yorkshire, Greater London and other large urban-industrial regions.[9]

---

7 Census of England and Wales, 1861, General Report, Appendix, 157.

8 Ibid., 156-7.

9 Before the 18th century areas in the West Midlands with the biggest population densities were fertile agricultural lowlands where, for

For the decade of the 1870s, E. G. Ravenstein found similar flows into Warwickshire from the nearby countryside and out again to the industrial North and to London.[10] Whatever the direction of population flows, the magnitude shows somewhat different results. Warwickshire provided 0.23 percent of the population in Yorkshire, 0.30 percent in Lancashire, 0.47 in Surrey, 0.71 in Middlesex, and 0.31 in Kent. Except for Kent and Surrey, however, those counties provided relatively more of the Warwickshire population: Yorkshire, 0.69 percent; Lancashire, 0.90; Surrey, 0.27; Middlesex, 1.86; and Kent, 0.27.[11] These results tend to confirm Redford's observation that most

---

example, were located Stafford, Lichfield, Warwick, Coventry, and Worcester. Lawton, "Population Movements in the West Midlands 1841-1861," Geography, 1958, 164-77. C. T. Smith noted that pastoral farming and urban markets greatly benefited agric lture in the Midlands and the North in the 1840s - 70s. London remained a great magnet, however. C. T. Smith, "The Movement of Population in England and Wales in 1851 and 1861," Geographical Journal, 1951, 200-10.Economic historians ought also take note of J. A. Banks' argument that sociological factors should also be considered in city growth: "Population Change and the Victorian City," Victorian Studies, March 1968, 277-89.

10 E. G. Ravenstein, "The Laws of Migration," Journal of the Statistical Society, June 1885, 194.

11 Census of England and Wales, 1861, 157.

migration was short-distance.[12]

Training

Although most migrants followed the general trend by coming to Birmingham from nearby farms and villages, patterns of long distance migration raise intriguing questions about the function of the hardware district in training an industrial labor force. Both Ravenstein and Lawton implied that people moved to Birmingham for initial training and then moved on to other areas either for more training or more money. The nature of hardware and metal working industries makes this suggestion even more plausible.

Because Birmingham had so many distinct industries even within the metal trades, a consciously developed training system would ensure that students learned common skills, which would make the labor market more flexible and prevent simultaneous oversupply in one industry with undersupply in another. Particularly in industries reputedly dependent on highly skilled labor, one would expect an articulated, comprehensive system

---

12 A. Reford, Labour Migration in England 1800-1850, 2nd. edn. 1926, edited, revised by W. Chaloner, A. Kelley, New York, 1968, 183.

of passing traditional skills from generation to generation. Yet, not only did the hardware industries as a whole fail to provide such an institution, but individual trades themselves rarely displayed comprehensive breadth or depth in instructing labor force entrants.

Because the Birmingham economy performed so many functions, one would not expect a single system to satisfy all needs, but no system at all seems to have existed. Indeed, extreme diversity characterized training in the city.

Like industrial organization in the city, the apprenticeship system in Birmingham had historical roots in the preindustrial world, specifically in Elizabethan legislation, which deserves brief mention.

Originally conceived as part of much broader social legislation, the Statute of Artificers of 1563 concentrated on regulating contracts for all labor, setting wages by justices of the peace, and regulating apprenticeships, the latter two measures being relatively new functions for the national government.[13] The government sought to do much with the law: quell social unrest, stimulate quality in industrial

---

[13] M. D. Davies, The Enforcement of English Apprenticeship: A Study in Applied Mercantilism 1563-1642, Harvard University Press, 1956, 1.

production (vital for export markets), care for the poor, and stimulate declining corporate towns by restricting apprenticeships to them.[14] Basically, the act required a seven year apprenticeship for industrial workers, who numbered relatively few in the 16th century.[15]

Not surprisingly, the law soon suffered evasion. Some masters bound apprentices even though they had no work, presumably to transfer them for a fee to masters who had work, but could only register a certain number of apprentices.[16]

By the early 18th century, the apprenticeship system held even less sway.[17] By the 1780s Coventry watchmakers reportedly taught their apprentices only a few of the many skills needed in this very specialized trade and released them with little useful training. Few boys actually lived with their masters.[18]

In the early modern period, before the widespread use of premiums, masters did not recoup training costs until late in apprenticeships, which explains, in part, the seven year

---

[14] O. J. Dunlop, English Apprenticeship and Child Labour: A History, Unwin, London, 1912, 61-2,66.

[15] Ibid., 60.

[16] Ibid., 127.

[17] Ibid., 224.

[18] Ibid., 231.

duration. (Although there are hints that such was the case also in 19th century Birmingham.) In the 18th century, however, premiums became common, prompting much complaint, and Parliament eventually repealed the statute in 1814.[19]

Although no evidence of gild control in Birmingham appears in the first half of the 19th century, some traditional labor institutions existed. Grounded in Elizabethan law, apprenticeship contracts existed between employer and employee associations but without comprehensive figures one can only surmise as to their prevalence.[20] Surprisingly, for a city reportedly employing much skilled labor, few apprenticeship documents survived, if, indeed, many were ever formally drawn up. If the average hardware worker had to meet certain skill requirements, one would assume that more than a handful of documents would now exist as witness. As noted, David Landes has remarked that perhaps over 80 percent of apprentices went to work without completing the full training term.

The few remaining indentures suggest that the apprenticechip "system" responded quickly to economic change. Masters transferred apprentices to other masters in the same or

---

[19] Ibid., 199, 61.

[20] Professor Robert Ozanne provided helpful insights on this point.

completely different trades, even after a boy had spent much time in "training." For example, in 1786, John Cash, "one of the Poor Boys belonging to Fantham's Charity in the Charity School of Birmingham," was indentured for seven years to Edward Piercy, a Birmingham stationer, bookseller, binder, and printer. The indenture was terminated four years later, however, and Thomas Ketland, a Birmingham gunmaker, indemnified Piercy "against all Costs Charges Damages and Expences by reason of the said Indenture and of the Release hereby made."[21] Presumably,Ketland needed labor and this transfer was an accepted was of getting it. In 1789 William Savage, a Birmingham bucklemaker, took on John Man to serve him as apprentice until age 21, but in 1791 assigned him to William Hand, another bucklemaker.[22] In 1788 William Smith took on Walter Showell to begin a seven year apprenticeship, but a year later, with Showell's consent, transferred him to Thomas Deakin, an upholsterer and cabinet maker, for the rest of the term. Showell

---

21 Lee, Crowder, Deposit, Apprenticeship Indentures, Box 22c-25, Birmingham Reference Library.

22 Ibid.

was to get 2s. 6d. a week his first year, rising to 8s. a week in his seventh.[23]

Unbound by tradition or sentiment, fathers sought to apprentice their sons most advantageously, even if outside the family trade.[24] Not restricted to apprentices, contracts for services appeared commonly between masters and journeymen and even between masters themselves.

In 1791 Benjamin Watkins, a journeyman buttonmaker agreed to work for three years for a buttonmaker (presumably a master) for 10s. a week the first year, rising to 12s. a week in the third and last year of the contract.[25] Yet two years earlier David Jones, also a journeyman (buckle and) buttonmaker, agreed to serve a partnership of button and bucklemakers for three years at twice the weekly wages.[26] Either the premium for superior craftsmanship was very high or

---

23 Ibid.

24 In 1791 William Ellis, a chemist, bound his son to a plater, for seven years. Ibid. In 1792 Nicholas Loft, son-in-law of a baker, apprenticed himself to a partnership of button-burnishers. Ibid. Documents reveal many similar cases.

25 Ibid.

26 Ibid.

Jones had assistants who would enable him to produce much more. The ambiguity surrounding the two cases illustrates the blurred distinction among labor services in Birmingham. Even though both Watkins and Jones were journeymen, not masters, no law or custom granted them the same wages for perhaps the same work. Although often called "servants" in contracts, many workmen (perhaps masters) were in far stronger positions than either Jones or Watkins. For example, in 1789 Thomas Elston, a Birmingham saddle tree maker, paid £15. 15s. 0d. to William Innis, a saddle tree maker, to be his servant for five years. Elston was to pay 6s. 6d. for each dozen "Beut" hunting tree saddles, 3s. per dozen hunting tree saddles, and 6s. 6d. for side tree saddles. Elston paid Innis 7s. per year for candles and allowed Elizabeth Innis, William's wife, "the priveledge and advantage of half of the canvassing of the work during the said Term of Five Years." Both Elston and Innis bound themselves £100 in case of default.[27]

Other agreements for labor services also existed in Birmingham in the late 19th

---

27 Ibid.

century. Thus in 1865 Thomas Wigley, a Birmingham gold and silver engraver, agreed to work for another gold and silver engraver for three years at 15s. a week guaranteed minimum plus overtime.[28]

In 1863 William Lyle, a thrower of stone ware, offered to manage and work for two years in the operations of William Bagnall, a potter with a works in Birmingham. Lyle received 36 shillings for a 60-hour week plus a bonus of 20 shillings a year. He had to "keep the books and accounts of the said Works Trade and business," take stock and wait on customers. Though Lyle got a house with a 3s. a week rental allowance, Bagnall could deduct the appropriate amount if he became sick or otherwise discontinued service before the end of the contract. No provision for profit-sharing appeared, leaving little doubt that this was a labor service rather than a partnership arrangement.[29]

Apprenticeships existed in a variety of employments, from least to most desirable, and apparently were customary for persons in all income levels. For example, in 1810 a Bilston printer advertised that female

---

[28] West Hagley Deposit, No. 258, Birmingham Reference Library.

[29] Ibid.

apprentices were needed in a manufactory, directing his information "TO PARISH OFFICERS."[30] More often, however, guardians of the poor from Birmingham and other cities ran their own ads, offering, occasionally with premiums, to set children out into apprenticeships.[31]

Evidently widespread, apprenticeships played varying roles: depending on the trade, master, and premium, they provided training, a relatively stable, low paid workforce, or capital (through premiums) to employers.

Like many facets of labor in Birmingham, no clear picture emerges. The system allowed much flexibility, for employers did not always take on apprentices for full terms. Apparently, age of majority was more important than years of service in gaining journeyman status, and a pool of unattached apprentices existed. Thus, the Kenrick and Bolton firm took on an apprentice plater for three years.[32] Even as late as 1850 a Birmingham employer could advertise for"a respectable Youth, from 16 to 18 years of age, to the Grocery and Provision Trade. One who has served part of his time would be preferred."[33]

---

30 Aris, April 30, 1810.

31 Ibid.,July 15, 1812; March 8, 1819, August 5, 1850.

32 Church, Kenrick, 23n.

33 Aris, May 6, 1850.

Geographically isolated labor markets within the same trade do not seem to have existed, and some trades, particularly services, consistently required high premiums, regardless of location.[34]

As suggested in the table below, premiums varied widely. Although applicable to London around the mid-18th century, the table provides some indication of entry requirements for various trades. Most Birmingham workers earned a pound or less a week and therefore a five pound premium could easily bar entry even to a trade with relatively low social and economic status.

---

34 *Ibid.*, November 13, 1809; April 13, 1801.

APPRENTICESHIP PREMIUMS FOR VARIOUS TRADES

Name of Trades	Sums given with an Apprentice £
Attorney	20 to 200
Baker	5 to 20
Bellows Maker	5 to 10
Brazier	5 to 20
Burnisher	5 to 10
_____ of Silver & Gold	5 to 10
Carpenter of Houses	10 to 20
Cheesemongers	5 to 50
Coach Makers	50 to 100
Coopers	10 to 20
Cutler	5 to 20
Enameler	10 to 20
Engine Maker	10 to 20
Edge-Tool Makers	5 to 10
Founders of Grates	10 to 20
Goldsmith	20 to 50
Grocer	20 to 100
Gun Smith	10 to 20
Haberdashers	10 to 50
Jewellers	20 to 200
Ironmonger	30 to 100
Linen Draper	20 to 100
Milliners	5 to 20
Mercer	50 to 200
Pattern Drawer	5 to 10
Plumber	10 to 20
Pin Maker	5 to 10
Screw Maker	5 to 10
Scale Maker	10 to 20
_____ for Files	to 5
Stationer	20 to 30
Surgeon	20 to 100
Taylor	5 to 10
Tobacconist	30 to 100
Wire Drawer	5 to 20
Woolen Draper	50 to 200

Source: R. Campbell, The London Tradesmen (1747), p. 331-340.

Even early in the century out-of-town employers looked to Birmingham for experienced workers and, less often, for apprentices. Offices of attorneys and others seemed to act as crude labor exchanges for various types of labor, but more often job seekers or offerers advertised directly.[35]

The only substantial evidence of apprenticeships in commercial enterprise in Birmingham appear in the wage books of the Scholefield-Goodman firm in the mid-19th century. Apprentices largely clerked in counting offices and warehouses. The company had no consistent policy for recruiting employees, although the work routine, pay, and promotion differed little after apprentices were taken on.

Scholefield-Goodman did not recruit apprentices actively, perhaps because of the small size of the permanent workforce and light turnover. Typically, apprentices came from families of friends or other businessmen.

---

35 Aris, November 8, 1819; June 29, 1818; November 3, 1800; April 27, 1801; April 20, 1801. Corroborating the high opportunity cost of training, some employers, especially those in remote areas, provided full family employment, as well as other amenities. For example, a mill near Derby seeking papermakers offered "Good wages for all Customs. . ., and Houses at moderate Rents will be found. . ., with constant Employment for Women and Children." Ibid., August 24, 1812. Women formed an important part of the labor

Rowland Richards, apprenticed in 1853 at age 15 at a beginning salary of 5s. per week, and discharged in late 1857 is a case in point. According to his record in the wages book, Richards had come to the firm from another enterprise and was known by one of the firm's employees. Nearly discharged in 1854 for "a want of strict truthfulness," he remained on until December 1857 when he was dismissed allegedly because of poor trade. Considering itself obliged to keep him until his 21st birthday, the firm kept him on until he found another position. Possibly the firm could legally have fired him for cause but might have wished to avoid unpleasantness because of ties with the boy's family.[36]

Several points emerge here. Richards had served at least some time with another firm, and was easily enough dismissed from

---

force and also fit into the traditional apprenticeship system. In 1812 an employer noted that she had "Vacancies for six young Ladies as in-door Apprentices to the Millinery and Dressmaking Businesses." Ibid., August, 24, 1812.

36 Scholefield, Goodman Collection, Item No. 10 Wages Book 1849-1872, University of Birmingham Library.

Scholefield-Goodman. His apprenticeship seemed in no way critical to the operation of the firm, although his duties were unspecified. Richards probably engaged solely in office work rather than in direct production activity. His apprenticeship was marginal to the firm, which by 1876 had a sales volume of over £100,000.[37]

Scholefield-Goodman seems to have had a fairly well-formed apprenticeship system.[38] Typically the firm advanced apprentice's wages to £80 a year upon reaching age 21, and occasionally put sons of friends to work at no salary simply to learn the trade or basic business practices.[39] For example, the firm took on William Kenrick in 1855 at age seventeen "with a view to fitting him for the future management

---

37 Scholefield, Goodman Collection, Box 2, Item No. 23. The documents are not clear, but it seems plausible to assume these are sales figures.

38 With the addition of fifteen year old Henry Smith, son of John Smith, a brassfounder, on March 10, 1859, the wages book notes "Salary to rise 1/. a year according to the usual scale - from a beginning salary of 5s. a week". Scholefield, Goodman Collection, Wages Book 1849-1872.

39 John Court, apprenticed in 1853 at the 5s. weekly salary, was advanced to £80 upon coming of age. He left, like many who had acquired the valuable experience, for another position: "to take a hardware agency in Birmingham for some London house." Ibid.

of his father's mining property."[40]

Terms of apprenticeship changed hardly at all by the late 19th century. Even in 1883, Scholefield-Goodman paid apprentices 5s. a week to start and still increased their pay only a shilling a year.[41]

Uncomprehensive and highly decentralized, the apprenticeship "system" was hardly a system at all, but rather an ad hoc contract of convenience available to employer and employees if they chose to use it. Although enforced by law like all contracts, apprenticeships in Birmingham were not controlled by labor organizations and thus did little to "stabilize" the labor market. In a few short-lived cases, journeymen organized to raise wages during the Napoleonic Wars,but did not try to alter apprenticeships.[42] The Birmingham Chamber of Commerce once expressed concern about inflexibility in the labor market because of apprenticeships but never mentioned the subject after the repeal of the Statute of Artificers.[43]

---

40 Ibid.

41 Scholefield, Goodman Collection, Item No. 101.

42 Aris, January 19, 1801; March 2, 1801; June 11, 1810; May 21, 1810; June 18, 1810; June 11, 1810.

43 Wright, Chronicles, 60-2.

Because contemporaries kept few records, of which even fewer survived, one cannot easily judge the effectiveness of training or even the percentage of youths apprenticed. No official or unofficial body kept count until trade unions became more organized later in the century. In some trades masters demanded exhorbitant premiums; in others, none at all. In some trades masters took great pains to instruct their students; in others, apprentices simply performed specific tasks for specified rates of pay, acquiring knowledge incidentally.

Money certainly brought advantage. Thus, S. W. Challen, whose father could afford to rent and work a 420 acre farm, became a premium apprentice in a small engineering works in 1856, found funds to buy one-quarter share of the much expanded firm in 1873, and became a full partner two years later. Even though apprentices accounted for four of the twenty workers in the firm in 1855, Challen seems to have received uniquely thorough instruction.[44]

In any event, no institutions either controlled or operated the system, suggesting a predominance of relatively low skill levels that inhibited organization.

---

44 S. W. Challen, "His Book," unpubl. MS, Taylor, Challen Collection, University of Birmingham.

Education

Not only did vocational training appear a checkered institution in Birmingham, but general education seems to have had the same qualities. No public institutions sought to provide fundamental reading, writing, or arithmetical skills to the young population at large, although private bodies set up schools and helped poor families with tuition payments. No national legislation on elementary education appeared until the 1870s, although weakly enforced early factory acts required schooling for factory children.

From the mid-19th century many studies found uneven educational quality in Birmingham. A study of 1373 working class children from ages seven to thirteen in the 1850s indicated that formal education lasted only a short while at best. Of all children in this age group, 38.5 percent were employed; of those aged nine and ten, 28.5 percent; ten and eleven, 44.5 percent; eleven and twelve, 73.5 percent; twelve and thirteen, 82.5 percent.[45]

---

45 William Gover, Our Work: or Remarks Upon the Results of "An Inquiry into the State of Education of the Children of the Working Classes in Birmingham, as Affected by the Demand for Labour, and by other Causes,"..., Simpkin and Marshall, London, 1857, Appendix, Table I.

Of employed twelve and thirteen year old children, just over ten percent attended day school but under three percent evening school.

Published in 1868, the first report of the Birmingham Education Society found the education of "the manual labourer and poorer classes" discouraging.[46] Of the 45,056 schoolaged children (beginning at age three) in Birmingham, 26,194 could neither read nor write; 5,482 could only read.[47] On average boys spent one and three-quarters years in school; girls, two and one-quarter.

Studying 908 factory workers ages 13 and 21 a committee of the Society found only 41 who passed a test of reading and writing a paragraph and doing simple arithmetic, although almost one-half had attended school for over three years.[48]

The factory acts made education mandatory for factory children, but exempted workshops with fewer than 50 people, and thus little affected Birmingham. Some contemporaries suggested that children fired by factories were hired by workshops, which provided even

---

46 Jesse Collings, "On the State of Education in Birmingham," Cornish Bros. Birmingham,1869, 3.

47 Ibid., 4.

48 Ibid., A night school for mechanics, The Midlands Institute, found it difficult to operate with people who lacked fundamentals. Ibid., 10.

less desirable employment and certainly no training opportunities.[49]

Paraphrasing Adam Smith's lectures on the social and psychological dangers of over-specialized, narrow work tasks, Edwin Cannan remarked:

> In Scotland the meanest porter can read and write, but at Birmingham boys of six or seven can earn threepence or sixpence a day, so that their parents put them to work early and their education is neglected.[50]

Poverty stunted school attendance. Of 300 families selected randomly from the 1842 persons receiving aid from the Society for the Improvement of Education to help pay school fees, the average income per head after rent was 1s. 1½d. per week, and only 31 children attended schools. Obviously most people could not afford the 2d. or 3d. per child per week school fees.[51]

Like vocational training, general education seemed hardly comprehensive even in the 1860s. No evidence indicates that Birmingham did better or worse than other cities in educating its young, and seemed to find jobs

---

[49] Ibid., 11.

[50] Adam Smith, The Wealth of Nations, E. Cannan. ed., xxxiii-xxxiv.

[51] Collings, "On the State of Education", 11.

for them with comparable efficiency. If training and educational opportunities were relatively few, jobs were not. A majority of the workforce in several industries, children paid high short run opportunity costs in attending school for any long period of time. According to the manager of an electroplating works interviewed by the Children's Employment Commission:

> . . . there is . . . so great a demand for young labour . . . that children are taken from school by their parents as soon as any employment can be got for them. . . .[52]

Clearly, unskilled and semi-skilled labor played no small role in the growth of Birmingham.

It seems inconsistent that an industrial system supposed to depend critically upon large numbers of skilled workers had such inadequate institutions to train them. The city itself did not assume responsibility for providing even basic skills until late in the nineteenth century. The fragmented process of learning reflected the diversity and nature of industry in Birmingham. Some apprentices received detailed, thorough instruction in mechanical arts, others served merely as low paid contracted labor. Although one cannot assert without qualification that Birmingham industry failed to train a highly skilled labor force, one cannot strongly assert the

---

[52] Children's Employment Commission, 3rd report, 1864, 123.

reverse, either. In Birmingham as elsewhere, some workers received superb training and developed into productive, creative journeymen and masters. There is no reason to believe, however, that such talent was typical. However well trained or educated on the margin, the Birmingham labor force showed no unique qualities on average.

CHAPTER SIX: SERVICES IN THE BIRMINGHAM ECONOMY

General Role of Services

Thus far, this study has focussed on labor forces in the manufacturing sector, seeking to emphasize the importance not only of primary sectors like textiles, iron, and coal but also of linked sectors like hardwares.

But manufacturing of any sort cannot exist in an economic vacuum, for goods must travel for processing, suppliers and buyers must pass information about prices, future orders, and credit, and goods must ultimately meet consumers at several loci for sale. In short, without auxiliary services like transportation, communication, and distribution systems, manufacturing cannot function as an activity integrated with its economic environment. As it grows more expansive and intricate, manufacturing requires even more services to keep account of and to manage its internal operation, to handle legal relations with other economic agents, and to pierce and develop new markets. As the variety of goods increases producers must develop more elaborate networks of wholesaling and retailing, including specialized advertising in the form of trade journals and directories, and new finance and insurance arrangements. Indeed, only through such services and intermediaries can manufacturing function as more than simply a production activity.

The implications for labor market analysis are not as obvious. Within services demand for and definitions of skilled labor differ enormously and linkages between service and manufacturing demands for labor are also ambiguous. Nonetheless, rapid growth of services in the early 19th century drastically altered the composition of output and undoubtedly affected labor markets as well, both positively and negatively. Workers producing fine wares benefited from increased incomes and growing numbers of retail outlets. Workers making outmoded buttons fared less well. Regardless of changes in direction for specific industries, the service sector deserves attention not only because of its own labor force but also because of changes it induced in manufacturing.

Despite its vital importance to growing national and urban economies, the service sector in general has not received much attention from scholars, and thus many questions of relative prices, productivity composition and size of output, and employment remain unasked.[1] In part because of such neglect, the complex process of urban growth, an integral part of the industrial revolution, eludes understanding. Although services provide perhaps the key point of tangency between the forces of urban growth and industrial growth, much research fails to integrate the two. Among the most widely discussed explanations of urban growth, central place theory places primary emphasis on services, while location theory considers only manufacturing.

---

[1] Some recent conceptual contributions include Colin Clark, Conditions of Economic Progress, 3rd. edn., Macmillan, London, 1957. P. T. Bauer, B. S. Yamey, "Economic Progress and Occupational Distribution," Economic Journal, December 1951, 741-55; A. G. B. Fisher, "A Note on Tertiary Production," Economic Journal, December 1952, 820-34; V. R. Fuchs, The Growing Importance of the Service Industries, National Bureau of Economic Research, Columbia UP, 1965, and his edited volume Production and Productivity in the Service Industries, NBER Vol. 34 Studies in Income and Wealth, Columbia UP, 1969, and The Service Economy, NBER, Columbia UP, 1968; George Stigler, Trends in Employment in the Service Industries, NBER, Princeton UP, 1956.; M. A. Katouzian, "The Development of the Service Sector: A New Approach," Oxford Economic Papers, New Series, November 1970, 362-82.; S. Kuznets, Modern Economic Growth: Rate, Structure, and Spread, Yale University Press, New Haven, 1966, 143-153; T. Weiss, "Urbanization and the Growth of the Service Workforce," Explorations in Economic History, Spring 1971, 241-258.

Pressing the industrial view, for example, P. Sargant Florence has argued that the location of manufacturing activity alone determines urban growth, and causes almost all urban economic problems. Thus, unemployment results from too little industry; overcrowding from too much. Unlike mining, agriculture, construction, utilities, and services, which must set up either where raw materials or populations exist, manufacturing enterprises are relatively footloose, and therefore cities grow only by attracting industry.[2]

Yet Florence uncritically generalized about plant mobility, failing to consider the depth of industrial roots in communities. Although some industries, like textiles, have historically relocated to more favorable tax or labor climates, other industries, like metal fabricating and tool making, have grown dependent on externalities like proximity to suppliers and markets, trained and retrainable labor, and social overhead like transportation. Thus, urban services like distribution, education, and transportation systems can themselves attract industry.

---

[2] P. Sargant Florence, Economics and Sociology of Industry, rev. edn., Johns Hopkins Press, Baltimore, 1969, 66-7.

Carrying this point even further, Eric Lampard emphatically argued that the urban area must offer services rather than manufacturing jobs as its main employment function. He reasoned that the progressive differentation of work involved in urban-industrial growth created productivity gains in primary and secondary sectors that freed workers for the tertiary sector. Cities grow because they offer specialization and economies of scale, especially external economies such as financial services, ready labor markets, and police protection.[3]

Thus, not only has overemphasis on textiles, coal, and iron hidden contributions of secondary industries like hardwares, but neglect of services betrays another blind spot in understanding the industrial revolution. Labor intensive by definition, services add a critical dimension to study of any urban labor force, such as that in Birmingham, experiencing rapid economic change. The service sector provides not only jobs but, more broadly, alternative employment opportunities which influence general wage rates.

---

[3] Eric Lampard, "The History of Cities in the Economically Advanced Areas," Economic Development and Cultural Change, January 1955, 101.

Historically less sensitive than manufacturing to depression, services provide more stable employment, and because of high skill requirements in many areas, services can boost average incomes.

As a diversified economy, Birmingham required several types of services, especially in transportation, finance, and distribution. The tertiary sector grew rapidly, particularly in the early 19th century and reflected as complex a mosaic of activity as manufacturing, with widely varying incomes and jobs. Surprisingly, tertiary activity in this major economic center has remained as unexamined as the city itself.[4]

Role of Services in Birmingham

Increasingly steadily in importance to Birmingham during the industrial revolution, services employed about forty percent of the

---

[4] Except for the following studies, which deal solely with distribution, virtually nothing has appeared on the historical development of services broadly defined for the British case: Dorothy Davis, *Fairs, Shops, and Supermarkets: A History of English Shopping*, University of Toronto Press, 1966; James B. Jefferys, *Retail Trading in Britain 1850-1950*, Cambridge University Press, 1954; Peter Mathias, *Retailing Revolution*, London, 1967; David Alexander, *Retailing in England during the Industrial Revolution*, University of London, Athens Press, 1970.

150,000 workers in 1861. The following table describes the situation more precisely.

Type of Service	# Occupied Persons
Public (civil)	770
Professional	3,630
Domestic	15,556
Wholesale, Retail, Communic., Transp., Ag.	33,516
Housing and Building	7,281
	60,753

Source: Census of England and Wales: 1861. My compilation and classification.

Although fairly aggregative, the table suggests several points. First, only about one-half of one percent of the occupied population worked for the civil government (national and local), somewhat under the national average and consistent with the negligible role played by the central government in developing the city.[5] The lack of public involvement in urban and industrial development in Birmingham

[5] C. Booth, "Occupations of the People of the United Kingdom, 1801-1881," Journal of the Statistical Society, June 1886, 415.

corresponded with the general policy outside London. Army purchases stimulated the gun trade in the city, and the Navy bought chains, ship sheathing and other goods, but most output went to private markets at home and abroad. Birmingham was not even the administrative center of Warwickshire, despite its overwhelming size. Government neither stimulated nor retarded the city, but simply ignored it.

Second, professionals accounted for only about two percent of the workforce, about the same as the national average, although expanding narrow 19th century definitions of the professions, which included lawyers, druggists, and music teachers but excluded accountants, factory managers, and bankers, might slightly alter the percentages.[6]

Third, domestic service (including more than the 8779 "domestic servants") claimed fully ten percent of the working population. Indeed, domestic servants outnumbered every other single occupational group in Birmingham and in the nation in 1861, although the national average was about fifty percent higher, suggesting perhaps the existence

---

[6] Ibid.

of more renumerative jobs for unskilled women in Birmingham.[7]

Nonetheless, the importance of such labor points to several phenomena. First, industrial change had yet done little to reduce labor requirements of household maintenance. Sturdier pots and pans, and other kitchenware, along with more durable beds, bedding, and garments had eased replacement needs but did not make cleaning or repair more productive. Second, the growth of incomes produced a middle class whose social standing, J. F. C. Harrison reports, depended on the size of its serving staff.[8] Indeed, domestics as a percentage of the national workforce increased throughout much of the 19th century. Rapid population growth and urbanization increased the number of households needing hired help and provided primary employment for unskilled female labor as well as part-time employment for other households. With high turnover rates and low pay, the market

---

[7] For the purpose of this paper, the "domestic classes" do not include wives not otherwise classified, although they did in the census itself. The figures cited above included only remunerated services. Also Booth, 415.

[8] J. F. C. Harrison, The Early Victorians 1832-1851, Weidenfeld and Nicholson, London, 1971, 109.

for domestics in Birmingham as elsewhere played a vital role in general employment.

Fourth, those in "Wholesale, Retail, Communications, Transportation, and Agriculture" comprised over 20 percent of the total labor force, roughly the national proportion if allowance is made for the greater influence of agriculture in national figures, and over half of the service labor force.[9]

Only about five percent of the total work-force (probably the same as the national average) and 11 percent of all service workers, those in transportation and communication reflected the diversity of the Birmingham economy.[10]

Unlike coal and iron sites, which require

---

[9] The "commercial classes" defined by the census included mercantile persons and "other general dealers," and numbered only 3915. Again problems are largely definitional. Newspaper agents were included under industry because they dealt with books. Tool makers and dealers were lumped together under industry, as were other dealers in most other industrial goods. It is of some interest that in a town of such size, only 139 persons (all men) listed themselves as "merchants;" only three as "bankers." Clearly small entrepreneurs performed many functions besides manufacturing. Quite likely they arranged for their own marketing and financing, at least. Also Deane and Cole, British Economic Growth, 142 and Booth, 415.

[10] No separate calculations for the communicatons sector exist. See Deane and Cole, British Economic Growth,142 and Booth, 415 to make rough estimates.

fairly simple transportation and communication networks, Birmingham made goods in several stages of production and at innumerable sites. Although transportation out of the city followed straightforward canal and eventually railroad lines, the considerable market in intermediate goods within the city called for substantial numbers of messengers, porters, errand boys, draymen,warehouse and storage workers.Generally involving little capital or skill, such activity employed a high percentage of women and children.

With nearly 20,000 workers, about one-third the service workforce and 13 percent of the total workforce, employment in wholesale and retail trade reflect the impact of population and income growth on Birmingham.[11]

---

11 The wholesale and retail group comprises a wide range of activities and had to be compiled from several categories. No attempt was made to segregate makers and dealers classified together in the census, but those performing service functions, though listed with industrial workers (like silk mercers), were included.Also included were more moot categories, like shoe and boot makers because they engaged in a local, consumer-oriented market and often performed maintenance functions like repair. Brewers were also included because they performed essentially a service function.

Notable here are the few who worked in public utilities. There were only 32 employees in waterworks service and only 207 in gasworks service.

Because technological and organizational change did not affect wholesale and retail trade until the late 19th century, jobs (including small entrepreneurships) in this sector often required much skill and paid commensurately.

Also critically dependent on population size and income, housing and building accounted for about five percent (slightly less than the national average of 5.8 percent) of the total workforce and about 12 percent of all those in services, and quite likely stood fairly high in average income.[12] Housing and building employed highly paid workers and included non-manual persons like house proprietors and agents, architects, surveyors, and builders.

A second source of data on service growth in Birmingham is the business directories cited earlier. Despite the failure to include attributes of firms, like number of employees, assets, and sales, the directories used more detailed activity classifications, providing a closer view of economic change. Covering years of rapid transition in Birmingham, the following table points to the growing importance of services among firms.

---

[12] Booth, 415.

All Activities	1830	1860
# types of firms	376	953
# firms	7709	19,774
Services		
# types of firms	99	247
# firms	3362	10,000

Thus, as both a percentage of types of firms and of firms themselves, the number of service firms grew faster than population, which doubled, and diversified more than other businesses.

Overall, the demand for professional services only kept pace with population growth. For example, the number of dentists remained fixed at 18, although the number of physicians increased from 9 to 19.

Surgeons increased from 71 to 160; professors and teachers from 41 to 73 (teachers only); and attorneys from 65 to 142 (141 solicitors; 1 barrister). Accountants break distinctively from this pattern, growing from 17 to 73, reflecting greater complexity of business operations, and increasing importance of large firms.

In contrast to the lackluster general performance of professional services, wholesale and retail trade experienced great absolute and relative changes, with far more specialization.

Some types of retail and wholesale trade made little relative headway, of course. Activities insensitive to economic growth, like pawnbrokers and furriers, either grew with or more rapidly than population but remained insignificant. Responding to deep-seated developments in consumer demand, other areas changed remarkably. Responding to income growth, for example, the 10 tobacconists and snuff dealers in Birmingham in 1830 grew to 173 tobacconists, two snuff box makers, and 25 snuffer makers in 1860. The number of grocers and tea dealers jumped from 128 to 446. In a similar vein, the 1830 directory listed 244 "shopkeepers and dealers in groceries, etc."; the 1860 directory listed 1207 shopkeepers.

Also responding to higher incomes, other food categories followed similar trends. The number of fishmongers tripled; the number of bakers quintupled. New functions developed in the food trade. There were no potato dealers and merchants listed in 1830; there were seven in 1860. No fish factors or herring merchants appeared in 1830; five of each existed in 1860. The 1860 directory even listed 220 farmers and 118 dairymen and cowkeepers, indicating the profitability of moving the farm to the market. Other functions, like those of provision dealers, factors, and merchants that did not achieve mention in 1830 appeared in 1860.

In nonfood areas roughly the same picture existed, with business growth generally greater than that of the population as a whole. In personal services, for example, chemists and druggists grew from 39 to 135; the number of clothes salesmen from 23 to 79. Stationers grew from 28 to 105 and 16 wholesalers had appeared by 1860. The 48 haberdashers of 1830 became 128 in 1860, including seven wholesalers.

Services then shared in and helped sustain the growth of Birmingham in the 19th century. Because most service enterprises were small, like some of their manufacturing counterparts, few records exist. Wage data appear even less often because pay was often determined by commission, a type of piece-rate. Service jobs competed with manufacturing for employees and offered a wide range of rapidly growing employment alternatives. As the city grew, linkages between services and other sectors of the diversified economy (like accountancy and manufacturing) grew more tighly bound and better integrated.

Thus, in a large and growing sector Birmingham demanded a high quality labor force, for nondomestic services generally remunerated well. Tobacconists, grocers, and tea dealers, for example, were small entrepreneurs who catered to well-heeled middle class customers. Wholesalers required clerks, warehousemen, commission agents, accountants, and other skilled employees to control internal operations, sell, and distribute goods.

The impact of growing service employment on the quality of the labor force in general and the hardware industries in particular is not clear, although at least one inference seems plausible. The growth of employment opportunities meant jobs for persons of all ages and skills, making Birmingham an attractive center for both workers and entrepreneurs. Tending local, regional, national, and international markets, by mid-19th century Birmingham had developed a labor force as highly diversified as its complex mix of commodity and service output. For entrepreneurs services might well have provided by 1860 the opportunity for mobility attributed to hardwares in 1777. As Chapter Two suggested, activities with the most firms probably had lower capital requirements, although, as with hardwares, only a few might have experienced meaningful mobility. Nonetheless, the rapid growth of shopkeepers of all sorts during the period attests to the importance of the service sector for entrepreneurs seeking advancement. By 1860 or even 1830, entrepreneurs in Birmingham or coming to Birmingham might have anticipated fewer difficulties in retail trade than in hardware manufacturers. At least they could expect more company.

CHAPTER SEVEN: URBAN-INDUSTRIAL GROWTH AND LABOR FORCE RECRUITMENT IN BIRMINGHAM: SOME CONCLUDING COMMENTS

Unfortunately, data do not allow firm conclusions about the nature of the labor force demanded during industrialization in Birmingham. Clearly, however, the stereotyped wall between Birmingham and Manchester suffers revealing chinks. If one cannot say with certainty that the hardware and textile industries employed the same quality of labor in the same quantity, one can assert at least that distinctions often seem to have few differences. Both industries employed only a fraction, albeit significant, of the respective labor forces. Both industries employed skilled, semi-skilled, and unskilled labor and both industries paid wages sufficiently high to attract workers from other occupations and areas.

Broad similarities in entrepreneurial environments also seem to have existed. In neither Birmingham nor Manchester were able workmen guaranteed success or failure in striving for greater social and economic status. Small firms thrived supplying the textile trade in Manchester and large firms garnered organizational and technological economies in the hardware trade in Birmingham.

Often more than two-thirds total costs in textiles, variable rather than fixed costs played a critical role in both Birmingham and Manchester, suggesting that talent, influence, and good credit ratings were important in both textiles and hardwares.[1]

What specifically attracted workers and entrepreneurs to Birmingham? Lacking adequate data one can only surmise, but some generalizations, tied closely to empirical evidence, seem warranted.

First, industrialization in the form of skill displacing technological change does seem to have occurred. Contemporaries like Martineau and Prosser expressed keen awareness of cumulatively significant advances in machine and hand-tool equipment. Along with such degradation of skill and increased specialization, however, grew the need for operatives, and women and children especially found jobs as machine watchers. More importantly,

---

1 Henry Ashworth, "Statistics on the present Depression of Trade at Bolton; showing the mode in which it affects the different Classes of a Manufacturing Population," Journal of the Statistical Society, April 1842, 74. See calculations of labor costs in Birmingham in the Appendix to the present study.

however, semi-skilled men found a ready if unsteady market for their hands.[2] This suggests simply that the demand for skilled labor seems to have grown less rapidly than the demand for unskilled and semi-skilled labor. Although based on partial evidence, wage data showing higher pay for laborers in Birmingham than in Manchester seem to reflect a relative shortage of unskilled and semi-skilled labor. Contemporaries also noted the availability of such jobs, and indeed, such a labor market might explain the disinterest of the Birmingham populace in social protest.

Second, barriers to mobility did not appear systematically lower in Birmingham than in Manchester. Although one must use partial evidence to question a hypotheseis itself built on partial evidence, it is necessary to assert at least that the issue remains unresolved. Considering data on capital structures, partnerships, and

---

[2] Although profitable for employers, child labor probably failed to return enough to parents to cover subsistence, as suggested by Wrigley. Most likely, families moved to areas where the male head of household could find employment, although jobs for women and children would offer even more attractiveness. E. A. Wrigley, Population and History, World University Library, London, 1969, 157.

public capital requests, the burden of proving mobility differences between Manchester and Birmingham falls on those hoping to find them. If Birmingham attracted entrepreneurs because initial fixed costs consumed so few funds, Manchester must also have attracted entrepreneurs for the same reasons.

Third, neither city seems to have had greatly differing occupational or wage structures, although Manchester might have paid more for skilled workers. Without knowing exactly how workers became skilled or to what degree Birmingham workers were more or less skilled than the workers in comparable categories elsewhere, one can make few irrefutable points. However, contemporary employers fully appreciated the lack of trade union strength, whether because Birmingham skilled workers had relatively fewer skills, or because the piece rate system precluded organization. In any event, employers seem to have faced few labor problems, making Birmingham a desirable refuge in a time of deep bitterness in labor relations.

The underlying issue remains the response of urban labor forces to the industrializing process. In Birmingham the bewildering diversity of output has for long disguised similarity of inputs. Birmingham attracted workers and entrepreneurs because they found the city more profitable than alternative locations. To assume, however, that the average immigrant to Birmingham differed radically from the average immigrant to any urban industrial complex in Great Britain seems to confuse average with marginal properties. Birmingham might have attracted a few critical skilled workers who gave the city a competitive edge in hardware production and distribution. One must seriously question, however, whether the average worker was of such unique importance. Far from remaining apart from the industrial revolution, Birmingham measured full strides in the march, flaunting familiar colors and strumming a common tatoo.

This confusion surrounding the responses of two different industrial systems to economic change in the same era suggests an even greater fogginess about the nature of the industrial revolution. As Lance Davis has recently noted, we do not yet have a workable definition of the industrial revolution, despite the man-years invested in describing its characteristics and consequences.[3]

We have discovered in this study aspects of the industrial revolution that affected two apparently quite distinct systems in much the same ways, through technological change, for example. We have also seen how the same two systems responded quite differently, in degree of social reaction to industrialization, for example. Yet we do not really know why increasing productivity, the key feature of industrial revolution, induced both similar and dissimilar results.

Many questions remain unanswered. If neither real mobility, high wages, nor economic instability were unique features of Birmingham, why did workers so rarely protest? Were they too poor to afford the risk? Did they face employers more powerful than textile mill owners? Did the piece rate system actually impede labor organization so effectively? Were employers more empathetic? More broadly, what exactly did the industrial revolution do to Birmingham?

---

[3] Lance Davis, "Specification, Quantification and Analysis in Economic History," G. R. Taylor, L. F. Ellsworth, eds., Approaches to American Economic History, University Press of Virginia, 1971, 109.

David Landes has discussed well the complexities of that economic upheaval, comparing its importance to neolithic man's first efforts to farm and husband and to specialize in tasks according to capacities.[4] Although we laud its performance, we still do not have a clear picture of what the industrial revolution did even to 18th century Britain. Were a stranger to inspect changes in occupational and output statistics, for example, he might devise two widely divergent interpretations, stressing gradualness from the former evidence and explosiveness from the latter.

Any suitable definition must clearly distinguish dependent and independent variables, for almost all discussions fail to specify the precise causal relationships. In this study we have investigated a uni-directional relationship - the impact of industrialization on an urban labor market. For a fully articulated insight into the relationship between industrialization and human resources we should take the next step and investigate the impact of an urban labor market on industrialization, for the quality and quantity

---

[4] Landes, Unbound Prometheus, 538.

of this vital factor of production can influence the nature, pace, and timing of industrial change. Entrepreneurs facing uncompetitively high labor costs will arrange their selection of technological and organization choices accordingly, for example.

Even after determining more precisely the causal relationships between industrialization and labor, economic historians must add a generally neglected dimension to their analysis. Although often discussed partially, the critical variable of space must be incorporated into models seeking to explain the industrial revolution. In a sense, of course, "industrial revolution" is a misnomer, for this basic restructuring of society occurred within a spatial as well as temporal context, that is, urbanization proceeded along with industrialization, feeding it and feed from it, but inseparable throughout. To paraphrase Galbraith, we live not in a new industrial state but in a new urban-industrial state. Unemployment in the city differs starkly from unemployment on the farm. In bringing people together in urban areas, industrialization not only occupied a workforce, but also created the problems of feeding, clothing, transporting, sheltering, healing, entertaining, and protecting it. Perhaps we will only understand this "urban-industrial revolution" of the 18th century with a fully developed systems approach that will clearly reveal the interdependencies of all relevant economic, political, social, and demographic variables and the degrees of their interdependencies.[5]

Until that time, however, we must begin creating the building clocks for that explanation with small but firm inquiries into pieces of that grand structure. Without a clear sense of direction, well-defined objectives, and a well-specified framework for analysis, we can expect to know only fragments of our past.

---

5 See a perceptive review in E. Lampard, "The Evolving System of Cities in the United States: Urbanization and Economic Development," H. Perloff, L. Wingo, Jr., eds., Issues in Urban Economics, Johns Hopkins Press, 1968, 81-139. See also H. J. Dyos' call for integrating business and urban history by focussing on the demand for labor in Urban History Newsletter, University of Leicester, Summer 1971, 3. For a broader perspective, see Dyos, "Agenda for Urban Historians," H. J. Dyos, ed., The Study of Urban History, Edward Arnold, London, 1968, 1-46.

APPENDIX

APPENDIX

Labor Costs

The diversity of occupations and industries in Birmingham was remarkable, and with such a dappled mixture, one expects the picture of labor's impact as a cost of production to show little consistency, and indeed the range is great. Labor costs in Birmingham fluctuated from nearly zero to over ninety percent of total costs in the case of some items, making average figures nearly meaningless without qualification.

The main sources of data are piece-work records for the pre-1850 period, mainly from the Boulton and Watt collection, and disaggregated cost data for custom-made engineering equipment for several firms in the 1880s and 1890s.

In these data, labor assumed from one-third to one-half total costs. Boulton and Watt had several systems of listing costs, generally separating wage and piece workers and providing itemized cost breakdowns for products. To fix profits, the firm fairly consistently marked up estimates by 33 percent but only on the labor component.

Presumably, the figure included overhead as well as profit because at this time estimates included only direct production costs. For example, the cost of a one-inch brass cock was broken down as follows: fitting, 25s.; one third the fitting cost (mark-up), 8s. 4d.; rough weight of cock (i.e., cost of raw material), 14s. 3d.; total estimate, 47s. 7d., rounded off to 48s.[1]

The same estimation procedure applied to all items, regardless of cost. For example, the total cost of a piece of machinery custom made in 1831 was £93. 7s.10d. of which fitting was £38.13s.8d. Exclusive of the one-third mark-up charged onto labor, the total labor cost was £29. 13s.5d., a little less than one-third total cost. Fitting included many operations, for example, boring, turning, drilling,and grinding, as well as the actual process of putting pieces together, and each had its own rate. In this particular case, boring and turning a cylinder was estimated to take five days at 15s. a day and fitting the cylinder 33s.9d. For all other parts,

---

[1] Boulton and Watt Collection, Room IX, Box 569, Estimates 1830-34, December 1, 1830, Birmingham Reference Library.

drilling would take three days and cost 24s., grinding two days and 30s., and "Labour" (undefined) four days and 12s.[2]

The separate piece-work accounts probably applied to outwork. For example, for the week of February 18 to February 25, 1842, Thomas Middleton received 10s. for "altering piston ring," 6s.3d. for "altering stand and core box for hand pump," and 21s.3d. for "making steam pipes for Messrs. Evans and Askin."[3] Quite likely, Middleton operated his own shop and worked not only for Boulton and Watt, but also for other engineering companies. Altogether seven piece-workers were listed as paid during that week, and there seems no reason why, if piece-work had been more important in terms of employing labor rather than other workshops, the figure should not have been much higher. The number of piece-workers fluctuated considerably, however. For example, only five were listed as paid during the week of November 14-25, 1845, compared with 12 for June 26 - July 3, 1846, and 18 for July 17-24, the same year.[4]

---

[2] _Ibid_., February 1831.

[3] Boulton and Watt Collection, Room IX, Box 559, Piece Workers' Ledger, 1842-1846, Birmingham Reference Library.

[4] _Ibid_.

By the 1880s and 1890s, labor remained generally one-third to one-half total costs but accounting systems for engineering firms became more detailed. For example, Taylor and Challen, a prosperous Birmingham engineering firm detailed costs for each item made, under the major categories of material, time, and trade expenses. The latter was neven defined, but probably included estimates for overhead and marketing, although items were generally custom made. Material and time expenses were broken down, but trade expenses remained an aggregate.

For example, the labor costs of building a steam engine in 1888 were:

Work Performed	Cost		
Patterns	£66	9	3
Turning, etc.	74	18	8
Slotting and Planing	37	3	11
Drilling	9	18	11
Fitting	74	15	6
Smith's Work	26	7	5
Drawing, Superintending, Office Expenses	16	7	0
	£306	0	4

The total cost of the engine was £951.9s.8d. Trade expenses were £183.9s.2d.;

material expenses, £462.0s.2d.[5]

The records of Charles Winn and Company provide even more detail, especially regarding day wages. Assuming a work week of 54 hours, weekly wages for boring and planing were 27s. (6d. an hour)[6] Painting, turning, fitting, and finishing paid 31s.6d. weekly (7d. an hour)[7] Slotting brought only 20s. a week (4d. an hour).[8] In 1884 turning, boring, drilling, fitting, painting, and finishing often brought 8d. an hour.[9]

---

[5] Taylor and Challen Cost Book, 22. Taylor and Challen Collection, University of Birmingham Library.

[6] S.W. Challen noted that the engineering work week in Birmingham dropped to 54 hours in 1872. S. W. Challen, "His Book".

[7] Charles Winn and Co. Collection, Machine shop cost book 1883-6, August 19, 1885, March 2, 1886, February 20, 1886. University of Birmingham.

[8] *Ibid.*, May 13, 1885. Some rates were actually higher in 1884 than in 1885, but it is not clear whether this anomaly was due to a change in average wages for all employees or to the use of less skilled labor in the latter year.

[9] *Ibid.*,September 18,1884, September 3,1884. In addition to its hourly wage system, Charles Winn and Company paid piece rates. For example, in the making of equipment in 1884 boring, tapping, and turning items were estimated at 6d. each, milling steel blocks at 2d. each, turning and cutting the screw at 4d.each. paint and painting at 1½d. each, and hardening blocks and finishing them at 4d. each. *Ibid.*, September 3, 1884.

Engineering was, of course, still highly labor-intensive near the end of the century. For example, a portable fire or garden engine with attachments cost £3.8s.7d. (which included 10 percent for "expenses"), of which labor cost 29s.1d., materials, 33s.3d. The sheer quantity of time needed to build the engine was considerable. Thirty-two hours were devoted to fitting alone, which cost 18s.8d.[10] Making a simple brass lining required 28 man-hours in turning, fitting, and boring.[11] Labor costs for this lining were 15s. out of a total labor and materials bill of 45s. Building a double ram pump with a steam cylinder required over 900 man-hours, not including piece-work. The total labor bill was £29.6s.8d. of which £3.14s.3d. was piece-work on which hours are unknown. Nine shillings of the piece-work bill went to another firm for planing. The total labor and material bill was £57.16s.4½d.[12]

Even though few wage data are comprehensive, wages in some industries seem to have

---

[10] Ibid., September 7, 1885.

[11] Ibid., November 23, 1885.

[12] Ibid., August 10, 1885. The planing figure was given only as a cost (£3.1s.0d.), which was converted to 122 hours by assuming a wage of 6d. an hour.

assumed from one-third to one-half total cost.

In contrast to the industrial sector, some service trades were less labor intensive. The first profit and loss account of the Birmingham Artisans' Club House Company, Limited, revealed total revenue of £1559. 5s.0d., of which only £171.8s.5d. went to labor. Food and groceries, the largest expense, took almost £1166. Profit was £22.11s.2d.[13] After 1876 wages and salaries were split and included with other expenses, precluding precise calculation. However, even in 1878 wages and incidental expenses and salaries and general expenses at the various coffee houses owned by the club cost about £2700, lagging far behind the £6800 spent for food and groceries. Total revenue that year was just over £12,700, of which £541 was profit.[14]

Because of the prevalence of piecework, rapidly changing output, and paucity of documentation, one can safely assert only that labor remained an important, if often indeterminate cost calculation for manufacturers in Birmingham.

---

13 Birmingham Coffee House Co., Ltd., Collection 1876, University of Birmingham.

14 *Ibid*., 1878.

BIBLIOGRAPHY

W. C. Aitken, "Brass and Brass Manufactures", _Birmingham and the Midland Hardware District_, S. Timmins, ed., 1866, A. Kelley, New York, 1968, 225-380.

David Alexander, _Retailing in England during the Industrial Revolution_, University of London, Athlone Press, 1970.

G. C. Allen, _The Industrial Development of Birmingham and the Black Country, 1860-1927_, George Allen and Unwin, London, 1929.

E. Ames, N. Rosenberg, "The Enfield Arsenal in Theory and History," _Economic Journal_, December 1968, 827-42.

S. L. Anderson, "The Attorney and the Early Capital Market in Lancashire," J. R. Harris, ed., _Liverpool and Merseyside Essays in the Economic and Social History of the Port and Its Hinterlands_, Frank Cass and Co., 1969.

T. S. Ashton, _An Eighteenth-Century Industrialist: Peter Stubs of Warrington 1756-1806_, Manchester University Press, 1939.

T. S. Ashton, _The Industrial Revolution, 1760-1830_, rev. ed., Oxford University Press, 1964.

Henry Ashworth, "Statistics of the Present Depression of Trade at Bolton," _Journal of the Statistical Society_, April 1842, 74-81.

Thomas Attwood, letter to Robert Peel in _Aris's Birmingham Gazette_, January 30, 1843, as found in F. W. Fetter, ed., _Selected Economic Writings of Thomas Attwood_, London School of Economics, 1964.

J. A. Banks, "Population Change and the Victorian City," Victorian Studies, March, 1968, 277-89.

G. J. Barnsby, "Standard of Living in the Black Country," Economic History Review, May 1971, 220-39.

P. T. Bauer, B. S. Yamey, "Economic Progress and Occupational Distribution," Economic Journal, December 1951, 741-55.

Brian J. L. Berry, Geography of Market Centers and Retail Distribution, Prentice-Hall, Englewood Cliffs, New Jersey, 1967.

Birmingham Public Libraries, Birmingham Before 1800, 1968.

Birmingham Statistical Society for the Improvement of Education, "Report on the State of Education in Birmingham," Journal of the Statistical Society, April 1840, 25-50.

Charles Booth, "Occupations of the People of the United Kingdom, 1801-81," Journal of the Statistical Society, June 1886, 314-417.

A. L. Bowley, Wages and Income in the United Kingdom Since 1860, Cambridge University Press, 1937.

Rhodes Boyson, The Ashworth Cotton Enterprise: The Rise and Fall of a Family Firm, 1818-1880, Oxford at the Clarendon Press, 1970.

Asa Briggs, ed., Chartist Studies, MacMillan, London, 1959.

Asa Briggs, History of Birmingham: Vol.II Borough and City 1865-1936, Oxford University Press, London, 1952.

Asa Briggs, "The Background of the Parliamentary Reform Movement in Three English Cities (1830-2)," Cambridge Historical Journal, 1952, 293-317.

Asa Briggs, The Making of Modern England, 1783-1867: The Age of Improvement, Harper Torchbooks, New York, 36-50.

Asa Briggs, "Thomas Attwood and the Economic Background of the Birmingham Political Union," Cambridge Historical Journal, 1948, 190-216.

Asa Briggs, Victorian Cities, Odhams, 1963 Penguin, London, 1968.

Asa Briggs, "The Victorian City: Quantity and Quality," Victorian Studies, Supplement, Summer, 1968, 711-30.

J. T. Bunce, C. A. Vince, History of the Corporation of Birmingham, 4 Vols., 1878-1923.

William A. Cadbury, Richard Tapper Cadbury, 1768-1860, Birmingham, 1944.

Rondo Cameron, ed., Banking in the Early Stages of Industrialization, Oxford University Press, New York, 1967.

Rondo Cameron, "England, 1750-1844," Rondo Cameron, ed., Banking in the Early Stages of Industrialization, Oxford University Press,1967, 15-59.

R. Campbell, The London Tradesman, 1747, David and Charles, Newton Abbot, 1969.

D. Chadwick, "On the Rate of Wages in Manchester and Salford, and the Manufacturing Districts of Lancashire, 1839-59," Journal of the Statistical Society, March 1860, 1-36.

W. H. Chaloner, "Writings on British Urban History 1934-1957, Covering the Period 1700 to the Present," Vierteljahrschrift fur Sociale -und Wirtschaftsgeschichte, March 1958, 76-87.

J. D. Chambers, The Workshop of the World, 2nd. ed., Oxford University Press, 1968.

J. D. Chambers, "Three Essays on the Population and Economy of the Midlands," Population in History, D. V. Glass, D. E. C. Eversley, eds., Arnold, London, 1965, 308-353.

Stanley Chapman, The Early Factory Masters: The Transition to the Factory System in the Early Factory System, Manchester University Press, 1958.

Stanley Chapman, "Fixed Capital Formation in the British Cotton Industry, 1770-1815," Economic History Review, August 1970, 235-66.

S. G. Checkland, "The Birmingham Economists, 1815-1850," Economic History Review, 1948, 1-19.

S. G. Checkland, The Rise of Industrial Society in England 1815-1885, Longmans, London, 1964.

S. G. Checkland, "English Provincial Cities," Economic History Review, December 1953, 195-203.

S. G. Checkland, "Toward a Definition of Urban History," The Study of Urban History, H. J. Dyos, ed., Arnold, London, 1968, 343-361.

Roy A. Church, Kenricks in Hardware: A Family Business 1791-1966, David and Charles, Newton Abbot, 1969.

Jesse Collings, "On the State of Education in Birmingham," Cornish Bros., Birmingham, 1869, 3.

"Contribution to the Economical Statistics of Birmingham," Journal of the Statistical Society, 1840, 434-441.

W. H. B. Court, _The Rise of the Midland Industries 1600-1838_, Oxford University Press, London, 1938.

M. G. Davies, _The Enforcement of English Apprenticeship: A Study in Applied Mercantilism 1563-1642_, Harvard University Press, 1956.

W. K. D. Davies, "The Ranking of Service Centres: A Critical Review," _Institute of British Geographers_, _Transactions_, December 1966, 51-65.

Dorothy David, _Fairs, Shops, and Supermarkets: A History of English Shopping_, University of Toronto Press, 1966.

Lance Davis, "Specification, Quantification and Analysis in Economic History," G. R. Taylor, L. F. Ellsworth, ed., _Approaches to American Economic History_, University Press of Virginia, 1971.

P. Deane, B. R. Mitchell, _Abstract of British Historical Statistics_, Cambridge University Press, 1962.

P. Deane, W. A. Cole, _British Economic Growth, 1688-1959_, 2nd. edn., Cambridge University Press, 1967.

P. Deane, _The First Industrial Revolution_, Cambridge University Press, 1965.

P. Deane, H. J. Habakkuk, "The Take-Off in Britain," W. W. Rostow, ed., _The Economics of Take-Off into Sustained Growth_, St. Martin's Press, New York, 1963, 63-82.

R. K. Dent, _Old and New Birmingham_, 1880.

R. K. Dent, _The Making of Birmingham_, London, 1894.

William Dugdale, _The Antiquities of Warwickshire_, 2nd. edn., 1730, Birmingham Reference Library.

K. Dunham, The Gun Trade of Birmingham, City of Birmingham Museum and Art Gallery, 1955.

D. J. Dunlop, English Apprenticeship and Child Labour: A History, Unwin, London, 1912.

H. J. Dyos, "Agenda for Urban Historians," The Study of Urban History, H. J. Dyos, ed., Arnold, London, 1969, 1-46.

H. J. Dyos, "The Growth of Cities in the Nineteenth Century," Victorian Studies, Vol. IX, No. 3, 225-37.

J. F. Edo, History of Wednesbury, Wednesbury Corporation, 1962.

F. M. Eden, The State of the Poor, 3 Vols., London, 1797.

D. E. C. Eversley, "Industry and Trade of 1500-1880," Victoria History of the Counties of England - A History of the County of Warwick, W. B. Stevens, ed., Vol. VII, The City of Birmingham, Oxford University Press, 1964, 81-139.

A. G. B. Fisher, "A Note on Tertiary Production," Economic Journal, December 1952, 820-34.

R. S. Fitton, A. P. Wadsworth, The Strutts and the Arkwrights, 1758-1830: A Study of the Early Factory System, Manchester University Press, 1958.

M. W. Flinn, British Population Growth, 1700-1850, MacMillan, 1970.

P. Sargant Florence, Economics and Sociology of Industry, rev. edn., Johns Hopkins Press, Baltimore, 1969.

P. Sargant Florence, Investment, Location, and Size of Plant, Cambridge University Press, 1948.

Alan Fox, "Industrial Relations in Nineteenth-Century Birmingham," Oxford Economic Papers, 1955, 57-70.

V. R. Fuchs, The Growing Importance of the Service Industries, National Bureau of Economic Research, Columbia University Press, 1965.

V. R. Fuchs, ed., Production and Productivity in the Service Industries, National Bureau of Economic Research, Vol. 34, Studies in Income and Wealth, Columbia University Press, 1969.

V. R. Fuchs, The Service Economy, National Bureau of Economic Research, Columbia University Press, 1968.

Elizabeth Gilboy, Wages in Eighteenth Century England, Harvard University Press, 1934.

Conrad Gill, "Birmingham under the Street Commissioners, 1769-1851," University of Birmingham Historical Journal, 1948, 255-87.

Conrad Gill, History of Birmingham; Vol. I Manor and Borough to 1865, Oxford University Press, London, 1952.

J. D. Goodman, "The Birmingham Gun Trade," in Timmins, 381-431.

William Gover, Our Work: or Remarks Upon the Results of "An Inquiry into the State of Education of the Children of the Working Classes in Birmingham, as Affected by the Demand for Labour, and by other Causes,"....., Simpkin and Marshall, London, 1857.

H. J. Habakkuk, American and British Technology in the Nineteenth Century: the Search for Labour-Saving Inventions, Cambridge University Press, 1967.

H. J. Habakkuk, P. Deane, "The Take-Off in Britain," W. W. Rostow, ed., The Economics of Take-Off into Sustained Growth, St. Martin's Press, New York, 1963, 63-82.

Charles Hadfield, British Canals, 2nd edn., A. M. Kelley, New York, 1966.

Charles Hadfield, The Canal Age, David and Charles, Newton Abbot, 1968.

Charles Hadfield, The Canals of the West Midlands, 2nd. edn., David and Charles, Newton Abbot, 1969.

H. Hamilton, The English Brass and Copper Industries to 1800, Longmans, Green, London, 1926.

J. L. Hammond, B. Hammond, The Skilled Labourer 1760-1832, Longmans, London, 1919.

J. L. Hammond, B. Hammond, The Town Labourer 1760-1832, Longmans, London, 1917.

T. Harman, Showell's Dictionary of Birmingham, Walter Showell and Sons, Birmingham.

J. F. C. Harrison, The Early Victorians 1832-1851, Weidenfeld and Nicholson, London, 1971.

William Hawkes Smith, Birmingham and Its Vicinity, as a Manufacturing and Commercial District, Birmingham, 1836.

William Hawkes Smith, Birmingham and South Staffordshire, London, 1838.

E. M. Hewitt, "The Gun Trade of Birmingham," Victoria History of the Counties of England: Warwickshire, Vol. II, 1908, 226-32.

E. Hobsbawm, "The Machine Breakers," "The Tramping Artisan," "The Labour Aristocracy in Nineteenth-Century Britain," "Custom, Wages, and Work-Load," Labouring Men, Anchor, 1967.

E. M. Hoover, The Location of Economic Activity, McGraw-Hill, New York, 1948.

W. Hutton, The History of Birmingham, 4th edn. 1809, 6th edn., Birmingham, 1835.

W. T. Jackman, The Development of Transportation in Modern England, 1916, Frank Cass, London, 1966.

J. Jaffray, Hints for a History of Birmingham, 2 Vols., 1857.

James B. Jefferys, Retail Trading in Britain 1850-1950, Cambridge University Press, 1954.

James B. Jefferys, The Story of the Engineers, 1800-1945, Lawrence and Wishart, reprinted by Johnson Reprint Corporation, New York and London, 1970.

B. Johnson, M. Wise, "The Changing Regional Pattern during the Eighteenth Century," Birmingham and Its Regional Setting: A Scientific Survey, British Assocation for the Advancement of Science, 1950, 161-86.

G. S. Johnson, "On the Benefit Building and Freehold Land Societies of Birmingham," Journal of the Royal Statistical Society, 1865, 507-517.

B. Johnson, M. Wise, "The Black Country, 1800-1950," Birmingham and Its Regional Setting, British Association for the Advancement of Science, Birmingham, 1950, 229-248.

J. Jones, "Report on the Iron Trade of South Staffordshire, 1865," in Timmins.

Everett M. Kassalow, "Labor in Development: A Critique of Some Current Concepts," Proceedings of the 22nd Annual Meeting of the Industrial Relations Research Association, 1969, 270-281.

M. A. Katouzian, "The Development of the Service Sector: A New Approach," Oxford Economic Papers, November 1970, 362-382.

George Kenrick, "The Organization of Education in Birmingham," George Auden, ed., A Handbook for Birmingham and the Neighborhood, Birmingham, 1913.

J. R. Killick, W. Thomas, "The Provincial Stock Exchanges 1830-1870," Economic History Review, April 1970, 96-111.

Charles P. Kindleberger, Europe's Postwar Growth:The Role of Labor Supply, Harvard University Press, Cambridge, 1967.

R. H. Kinvig, "Introduction," Birmingham and Its Regional Setting: A Scientific Survey, British Association for the Advancement of Science, Birmingham, 1950, xv-xix.

Simon Kuznets, Modern Economic Growth, Yale University Press, New Haven, 1966, 86-159.

Eric Lampard, "The Evolving System of Cities in the United States: Urbanization and Economic Development," H. Perloff, L. Wingo, Jr., eds., Issues in Urban Economics, Johns Hopkins Press, 1968, 81-139.

Eric Lampard, "The History of Cities in the Economically Advanced Areas," Economic Development and Cultural Change, January 1955, 81-136.

David Landes, The Unbound Prometheus: Technological Change and Industrial Development in Western Europe from 1750 to the Present, Cambridge University Press, 1970.

John Langford, A Century of Birmingham Life, or a Chronicle of Events from 1741 to 1841, 2nd. edn., W. G. Moore, Birmingham, 2 Vols., 1870, 1871.

J. A. Langford, C. S. Mackintosh, J. C. Teldesley, Staffordshire and Warwickshire, Past and Present, 2 Vols., London, 1870.

S. Langley, "The Wednesbury Tube Trade," University of Birmingham Historical Journal, Vol. II, 1949-50, 163-77.

C. Law, "The Growth of Urban Population in England and Wales, 1801-1911," Institute of British Geographers, Transactions, June 1967, 125-43.

F. W. Lawrence, Local Variations in Wages, Longmans, Green, London, 1899.

R. Lawton, "Population Changes in England and Wales in the later 19th Century: An Analysis of Trends by Registration Districts," Institute of British Geographers, Transactions, May 1968, 55-74.

R. Lawton, "Population Movements in the West Midlands 1841-1861," Geography, 1958, 164-77.

Leone Levi, Wages and Earnings of the Working Classes, 1867.

Harold C. Livesay, Glenn Porter, "The Financial Role of Merchants in the Development of U.S. Manufacturing, 1815-1860," Explorations in Economic History, Fall 1971, 63-87.

Samuel Lloyd, The Lloyds of Birmingham, 3rd edn., 1909.

John Lord, Capital and Steam Power 1750-1800, P. S. King and Son, London, 1923.

C. S. Mackintosh, J. A. Langford, J. C. Teldesley, Staffordshire and Warwickshire, Past and Present, 2 Vols., London, 1870.

Paul Mantoux, The Industrial Revolution in the Eighteenth Century, rev. ed., Harper Torchbooks, New York, 1961.

Leon S. Marshall, "The English and American Industrial City of the Nineteenth Century," Western Pennsylvania Historical Magazine, September 1937, 169-80.

Peter Mathias, The First Industrial Nation, Methuen, London, 1969.

Peter Mathias, Retailing Revolution, Longmans, 1967.

William Matthews, A Sketch of the Principal Means Which Have Been Employed to Ameliorate the Intellectual and Moral Condition of the Working Classes at Birmingham, 1830, Birmingham Reference Library.

P. W. Matthews, compiler, Anthony W. Tuke, editor, History of Barclays Bank, Limited, Blades, East and Blades, London, 1926.

B. R. Mitchell, P. Deane, Abstract of British Historical Statistics, Cambridge University Press, 1962.

National Association for Promotion of Social Science, Trades' Societies and Strikes, London, 1860, reprinted by A. M. Kelley, New York, 1968.

R. S. Neale, "Standard of Living, 1780-1844: Regional and Class Study," Economic History Review, 1966.

Jane E. Norton, Guide to the National and Provincial Directories of England and Wales, Excluding London, published before 1856, Royal Historical Society Guides and Handbooks No. 5, London, 1950.

R. Padley, "The Beginnings of the British Alkali Industry," *University of Birmingham Historical Journal*, Vol. III, 1951-2, 64-78.

R. Pelham, "The Water-Power Crisis in Birmingham in the Eighteenth Century," *University of Birmingham Historical Journal*, Vol. IX, 1963, 64-91.

R. Pelham, "The West Midland Iron Industry and the American Market in the 18th Century ," *University of Birmingham Historical Journal*, Vol. II, 1949-50, 141-62.

R. Pelham, "The Worcester and Birmingham Canal," *University of Birmingham Historical Journal*, Vol. V, 1955, 60-82.

E. H. Phelps Brown, *A Century of Pay*, St. Martin's Press, New York, 1968.

G. Piggott, "Boiler Plate Working," in Timmins.

S. Pollard, *Genesis of Modern Management*, Harvard University Press, 1965, 160-208.

S. Pollard, *A History of Labour in Sheffield*, Liverpool University Press, 1959.

Glenn Porter, Harold C. Livesay, "The Financial Role of Merchants in the Development of U.S. Manufacturing, 1815-1860," *Explorations in Economic History*, Fall 1971, 63-87.

G. R. Porter, *The Progress of the Nation*, rev. by F. W. Hirst, Methuen, London, 1912, 1951.

L. S. Pressnell, *Country Banking in the Industrial Revolution*, Oxford University Press, London, 1956.

John Prest, *The Industrial Revolution in Coventry*, Oxford University Press, 1960.

Joseph Priestly, Historical Account of the Navigable Rivers, Canals, and Railways throughout Great Britain, 1st edn., 1831, 2nd edn., n.d., Frank Cass, 1967.

R. B. Prosser, Birmingham Inventors and Inventions, "Journal" Printing Works, Birmingham, 1881, Birmingham Reference Library.

E. G. Ravenstein, "The Laws of Migration," Journal of the Statistical Society," June 1885, 167-227.

P. Razzell, "Population Growth and Economic Change in Eighteenth-and Early Nineteenth-Century England and Ireland," E. Jones, G. Mingay, eds., Land, Labour, and Population in the Industrial Revolution, Barnes and Noble, New York, 1968, 260-81.

A. Redford, Labour Migration in England, 1800-1850, 1926, 2nd. edn., edited, revised by W. Chaloner, A. Kelley, New York, 1968.

Henry Rees, "Birmingham and the Black Country," Economic Geography, 1946, 133-41.

W. Rimmer, "The Industrial Profile of Leeds, 1740-1840," Publications of the Thoresby Society, Vol. L, Pt. 2, No. 113, 1967, 130-57.

W. Rimmer, "Occupations in Leeds, 1841-1951," Publications of the Thoresby Society, Vol. L, Pt. 2, No. 113, 1967, 158-78.

E. Roll, An Early Experiment in Industrial Organization, Being a History of the Firm of Boulton and Watt, 1775-1805, Longmans, Green, London, 1930.

N. Rosenberg, ed., The American System of Manufactures, Edinburgh University Press, 1969, 1-86.

N. Rosenberg, E. Ames, "The Enfield Arsenal in Theory and History," Economic Journal, December 1968, 827-42.

W. Ryland, "The Plated Wares and Electroplating Trades," S. Timmins, ed., Birmingham and the Midlands Hardware District, 1866, A. Kelley, New York, 1968.

W. L. Sargant, "On the Vital Statistics of Birmingham and Seven Other Large Towns," Journal of the Statistical Society, March 1866, 92-111.

C. Savage, An Economic History of Transport, Hutchinson, London, 1959.

Richard S. Sayers, Lloyds Bank in the History of English Banking, Oxford at the Clarendon Press, 1957.

Robert Schofield, The Lunar Society of Birmingham, Oxford at the Clarendon Press, 1963.

L. Schnore, "Problems in the Quantitative Study of Urban History," H. Dyos, ed., The Study of Urban History, Arnold, London, 1968, 189-208.

Showell's Dictionary of Birmingham, T. Harmon, compiler, Birmingham, 1885.

A. E. Smailes, "The Urban Hierarchy in England and Wales," Geography, June 1944, 41-51.

A. E. Smailes, "The Urban Mesh of England and Wales," Institute of British Geographers, Transactions, 1946, 87-101.

Adam Smith, An Inquiry into the Nature and Causes of the Wealth of Nations, E. Cannan, ed., Modern Library, 1937.

C. T. Smith, "The Movement of Population in England and Wales in 1851 and 1861," Geographical Journal, 1951, 200-210.

Roger Smith, "Demography in the Nineteenth Century: An Introduction for the Local Historian," The Local Historian, February 1970, 27-35.

Frederick W.Spackman, An Analysis of the Occupations of the People, M. Kelley, New York, 1847, 1969.

W. B. Stephens, ed., The Victoria History of the County of Warwick, Vol. VII: The City of Birmingham, 1964.

George Stigler, "The Division of Labor is Limited by the Extent of the Market," Journal of Political Economy, June 1951, 185-93.

George Stigler, Trends in Employment in the Service Industries, National Bureau of Economic Research, Princeton University Press, 1956.

A. Taylor, "The Sub-Contract System in the British Coal Industry," L. Pressnell, ed., Studies in the Industrial Revolution, Athlone Press, 1960, 215-35.

A. J. Taylor, "Concentration and Specialization in the Lancashire Cotton Industry, 1825-1850," Economic History Review, 1949, 114-122.

T. Tholfsen, "The Artisan and the Culture of Early Victorian Birmingham," University of Birmingham Historical Journal, Vol. IV, 1953-4, 146-66.

T. Tholfsen, "The Chartist Crisis in Birmingham," International Review of Social History, 1958, 461-80.

W. Thomas, J. R. Killick, "The Provincial Stock Exchanges 1830-1870," Economic History Review, April 1970, 96-111.

E. Thompson, The Making of the English Working Class, Gollancz, London, 1963.

W. R. Thompson, A Preface to Urban Economics, Johns Hopkins Press, Baltimore, 1965.

P. O. N. Thorpe, M. J. Wise, "The Growth of Birmingham, 1800-1950," Birmingham and Its Regional Setting: A Scientific Survey, British Association for the Advancement of Science, Birmingham, 1950, 213-228.

S. Timmins, "Birmingham in 1800," Birmingham Archaeological Society Transactions, 1888, 1-9.

S. Timmins, "The Industrial History of Birmingham," in Timmins, 207-224.

S. Timmins, ed., The Resources, Products, and Industrial History of Birmingham and the Midland Hardware District, 1866, A. M. Kelley, New York, 1968.

Anthony W. Tuke, editor, P. W. Matthews, compiler, History of Barclays Bank, Limited, Blades, East and Blades, London, 1926.

J. P. Turner, "The Birmingham Button Trade," in Timmins.

Urban History Newsletter, Summer 1971.

C. A. Vince, J. T. Bunce, History of the Corporation of Birmingham, 4 Vols., 1878-1923.

A. P. Wadsworth, R. S. Fitton, The Strutts and the Arkwrights, 1758-1830: A Study of the Early Factory System, Manchester University Press, 1958.

J. E. Wadsworth, W. F. Crick. A Hundred Years of Joint Stock Banking, Holder and Stoughton, London, 1936.

Benjamin Walker, "Birmingham Directories," Birmingham Archaelogical Society Transactions, 1937, 1-36.

A. Weber, Growth of Cities in the Nineteenth Century, MacMillan, New York, 1899.

F. A. Wells, Hollins and Viyella: A Study in Business History, A. M. Kelley, New York, 1968.

Thomas Weiss, "Urbanization and the Growth of the Service Workforce," Explorations in Economic History, Spring 1971, 241-58.

Iolo A. Williams, The Firm of Cadbury 1831-1931, London, 1931.

R. B. Wilson, "The Evolution of Local History Writing on Warwickshire," Birmingham Archaeological Society, Transactions, 1955, 63-75.

M. Wise, "Birmingham and Its Trade Relations in the Early 18th Century," University of Birmingham Historical Journal, Vol. II, 1949-50, 53-79.

M. Wise, B. Johnson, "The Changing Regional Pattern during the Eighteenth Century," Birmingham and Its Regional Setting: A Scientific Survey, British Association for the Advancement of Science, 1950, 161-86.

M. Wise, B. Johnson, "The Black Country, 1800-1950," Birmingham and Its Regional Setting, British Association for the Advancement of Science, 1950, 229-248.

M. J. Wise, "On the Evolution of the Jewellery and Gun Quarters in Birmingham," Institute of British Geographers, Transactions, 1949, 59-72.

M. J. Wise, "Some Factors Influencing the Growth of Birmingham," Geography, 1948, 176-90.

M. J. Wise, P. O. N. Thorpe, "The Growth of Birmingham, 1800-1950," Birmingham and Its Regional Setting: A Scientific Survey, British Association for the Advancement of Science, Birmingham, 1950, 213-228.

C. J. Woodward, "Birmingham Trades and Industries during the Last Century," Birmingham Archaeological Society, Transactions, 1905, 36-46.

J. Skirrow Wright, "An Account of Some New Trades in Birmingham, and Phases of its Social Life since 1832," Transactions of the National Association for the Promotion of Social Science, 1863, 826-32.

G. Henry Wright, Chronicles of the Birmingham Chamber of Commerce, Birmingham, 1913.

J. S. Wright, "The Jewellery and Gilt Toy Trades," in Timmins.

E. A. Wrigley, Population and History, World University Library, London, 1969, 145-202.

Newspapers

Aris' Birmingham Gazette, 1741-1861.

Birmingham Advertiser, 1836-1844.

Birmingham Journal

Swinney's Birmingham and Stafford Chronicle, 1775-1820, Birmingham Reference Library.

Wolverhampton Chronicle and Staffordshire Advertiser, Wolverhampton Reference Library.

Government Documents

"Abstract . . . of the Answers and Returns . . ." Parliamentary Papers, 1801, VI.

"Abstract of the Answers and Returns . . . ." 1831 Census, Parliamentary Papers, 1833, XXXVI-XXXVIII.

"Abstract of the Answers and Returns . . . , Occupation Abstract, 1841," Parliamentary Papers, 1844, XXVII.

Board of Trade, Return of Wages published between 1830 and 1886, 1887.

Census of England and Wales, 1861.

Census of Great Britain 1841: Occupational Abstract, 192-99.

E. Cheshire, The Results of the Census of Great Britain in 1851 with a Description of the Machinery and Processes Employed to Obtain the Returns, Parker and Sons, London, 1854.

Children's Employment Commission Reports, 1842, 1864.

"Comparative Account of the Population of Great Britain in the Years 1801, 1811, 1821, and 1831 . . . ," Parliamentary Papers, 1831, XVIII.

Factory Inquiries Commission, First Report of the Central Board. . as to the Employment of Children in Factories. . .with Minutes of Evidence and Reports by the District Commissioners, 28 June 1833, A. M. Kelley, New York, 1968.

House of Commons, Parliamentary Papers, Select Committee on Artizans and Machinery, 1924, in Six Reports from the Select Committee on Artizans and Machinery 23 February - 21 May 1824, Augustus M. Kelley, New York, 1968.

House of Commons, "Petitions Against Orders in Council,"1812.

Interdepartmental Committee on Social and Economic Research, Guide to Official Sources: No. 1, Labour Statistics, rev. ed., London, 1958.

"Summary of Answers and Returns . . . Occupations of . . . Families . . . and the Total Number of Males as Enumerated in the Years 1801, 1811, 1821, and 1831," Parliamentary Papers, 1833, V.

Archival Materials

Amalgamated Society of Engineers Monthly Report, July 1859, item HM 1331, University of Birmingham.

Birmingham Parish, Poor Rate Levy Book, 54 Vols., 1736-1843, Birmingham Reference Library.

Birmingham Coffee House Company, Ltd., Collection, University of Birmingham.

Boulton and Watt Collection, Birmingham Reference Library.

Chance and Homer Collection, University of Birmingham.

Coal Company (Birmingham) Records of the Birmingham Coal Company, 1. Minutes of Annual General Meetings, 1794 (45?) - 1862, Birmingham Reference Library.

Directories,

Bailey's Western and Midland Directory, 1783.

Bentley's History, Guide, and Alphabetical and Classified Directory, n.d. (These books existed for several areas.)

Chapman's Annual Directory, 1808.

New Triennial Directory of Birmingham, Thomson and Wrightson, 1808.

Pigot and Co.'s National Commercial Directory, 1835.

Pigot and Co.'s National Commercial Directory for 1828-9.

Pigot and Co.'s New Commercial Directory for Staffordshire, Warwickshire, Worcestershire, Shropshire and North Wales, 1829.

Post Office Directory of Birmingham, Kelley, London, 1860.

Post Office Directory of Birmingham, Staffordshire, Warwickshire, and Worcestershire for 1864, Kelley, 1863.

Charles Pye, A Description of Modern Birmingham, 1818.

Charles Pye, A New Directory for the Town of Birmingham and the Hamlet of Deritend, Pearson and Rollason, 1785.

Charles Pye, Pye's Birmingham Directory for the Year 1797.

Charles Pye, The Birmingham Directory for the Year 1788.

Charles Pye, The Stranger's Guide to Modern Birmingham, 1835.

John S. Roper, Wolverhampton: A List of Trades and Occupations from the Town Rate Book 1792, Geography Department, University of Birmingham, 1964.

Charles E.Scarse, complier and editor, Birmingham 120 Years Ago, 1896.

Sketchley's and Adams' True Guide, 4th edn., 1770.

Sketchley's Birmingham, Wolverhampton, and Walsall Directory, 1767.

Swinney's Birmingham Directory, 1777.

The Birmingham Directory, Pearson and Rollason, 1777.

The Birmingham, Wolverhampton, Walsall, Dudley, Bilston, and Willenhall Directory, Pearson and Rollason, 1781.

Universal British Directory of Trade, Commerce, and Manufacture, 1791.

William West, The History, Topography, and Directory of Warwickshire, R. Wrightson, 1830.

Francis White and Company, History, Gazetteer, and Directory of Warwickshire, 1850.

William White, History, Gazetteer, and Directory of Staffordshire, 1834.

Wrightson's New Triennial Directory of Birmingham, 1815.

Wrightson's Triennial Directory of Birmingham, 1825.

Ledger of Samuel Thornley of Snow Hill, Birmingham, dry salter, 1795-1805, Warwickshire County Record Office.

Lee, Crowder Collection, Partnership Deeds of Birmingham Firms, 1783-1825, and Apprenticeship Indentures, Birmingham Reference Library.

List of the Poor Belonging to Birmingham, 1766, 1781, 1784, 1786, 1788-9, 1790, 1822, Birmingham Reference Library.

Harriet Martineau Collection, University of Birmingham.

Prospectus for Establishing a Commercial Bank in Birmingham, 1829, Birmingham Reference Library.

Report by the Directors of the Bank of Birmingham to the Proprietors Assembled at the First Yearly General Meeting, Birmingham, 1833, Birmingham Reference Library.

Scholefield, Goodman Collection, University of Birmingham.

J. and C. Sturge's Corn Circular, 1833-87.

Taylor, Challen Collection, University of Birmingham.

Samuel Webb and Company Collection, University of Birmingham.

West Hagley Deposit, Partnership Indentures and Apprenticeship Indentures, Birmingham Reference Library.

Charles Winn and Company, University of Birmingham.